THE CHARACTER QUAD

A WRITER'S GUIDE TO
CREATING YOUR UNIVERSE

CHARLES A CORNELL

ASTRA
NOVELLUS LLP

EPWORTH, ENGLAND

Publisher: Astra Novellus Ltd
Email: astranovellus@runbox.com

Fair Use Statement: The author is aware some content in this writer's guide references copyrighted materials. The author asserts his right of fair use of this material for the purpose of critiquing or reviewing the copyright owners' original work and to provide examples of their work to demonstrate specific points. The provisions of fair use (USA) and of fair dealing (UK) allow such copyrighted material to be used for the purposes of criticism, commentary, or discussion of the work itself as long as the appropriate acknowledgement has been made to identify the creator of the work and the title of the material.

Book Cover Design by Charles A Cornell.
Graphics licensed from Shutterstock.com or obtained from public domain sources.

The Character Quad/ Charles A Cornell -- 1st ed.
ISBN 978-0-9990889-6-8

THE CHARACTER QUAD

Acknowledgments...4

What's the Problem?..5

Babies, Bathwater, and Textbooks 13

The Hero's Journey and The Big Bang 21

Defining Power & Wisdom 29

The Character Quad - The Basics 43

The Character Quad - Wizard of Oz 55

The Quad's Law of Relativity 73

Underdogs..77

Overlords...83

Mentors 93

Underlings 103

Character Arcs and The Quad 109

Conflicts and The Quad 131

Parachuting an Archetype into The Quad 147

Summary - Final Words 165

The Character Quad Template 169

Book Two: Exploring the Quad 171

Recommended Reference Texts 173

About the Author – Charles A Cornell 174

Fiction by Charles A. Cornell 175

Acknowledgments

A guide for writers is not much use unless it has passed the most critical test of all—do successful authors believe The Character Quad provides value, not only to those just starting out on their writing journey but also for those who have experienced many heartaches as they've tried to get their characters 'just right'?

I'm indebted to the insightfulness of authors Ken Pelham, Kristin Durfee, and Elle Andrews Patt for their patient critique of this new tool, The Character Quad. Their many suggestions and fine examples have added some necessary polish and clarity. Thank you!

CHAPTER ONE

What's the Problem?

Characters.

Readers love them. Readers hate them. And they should. That's what characters do—boil up emotion in us, one way or the other.

After all, that's the essence of story—to illicit an emotional response in the reader.

Events can illicit an emotional response—wars, natural disasters, the sinking of the Titanic. Your plot can do that—serial killers on the loose, a spooky haunting, spies exchanged at midnight on a bridge. If someone tells us about a tragedy we feel sad. If we read bad news we can become anxious and fearful. But there's nothing that invests the reader more in your story than experiencing those emotions through the eyes of your characters.

Whatever story you wish to tell, at the end of the day, how your readers view your characters will determine if they like your story or not. Of course, *how* you tell it—your craft—will be a big deciding factor too. A poorly written plot with ill-defined, emotionless characters will not inspire anyone. One star review, guaranteed.

I don't know many fictional novels whether literary or genre that have been written without characters. What story would they tell? Okay, that doesn't take too much convincing on my part. Your story has to have interesting characters. It's decided. *Phew*—glad we got that out of the way.

So, let's get started. You can't look at solutions if you don't know what the problem is.

Here's the problem:

There's a story buzzing in your head. Maybe it's like viewing a movie—your imagination runs wild as you sit with popcorn and take it all in. You see what's going on, where it's taking place, what century, what year. As the movie unfolds, you meet your first character, usually but maybe not always, the protagonist. You assign a gender, imagine a face, create an image of their life—how they dress, their background—whatever fits the story.

You start plotting (or simply start writing freestyle, the infamous 'pantser' technique) and *voila*—more characters pop into your head.

There has to be a villain, right? Of course, there does. A wicked stepmother. A robber baron. Scrooge.

And then, as if by magic, your hero or heroine is surrounded by people that love her, that guide her, that protect her.

But suddenly, the bad guy (or girl) is surrounded by their own cast of supporting acts—accomplices of all kinds that thwart your protagonist's progress on their quest. A black knight. The godfather's hit man. The galactic bounty hunter. The corrupt tax collector or mean sheriff.

You have to counteract that evil, don't you? You grow more characters on the side of good. It's your imagination, so who's going to stop you? And soon, a battle royal results between good and evil. Your story is so full of characters, it's getting out of control!

You seek help.

There must be an answer to resolve the absolute chaos you've created. You're confused and you want guidance. You become your own protagonist on a quest for sanity. Your solution? You buy a book on writing characters.

In my case I bought four.

It was more than twenty years ago and I'm still learning how to write characters. The truth is, you never stop learning how to write and that means you're always buying books on 'how to write', even if you've already done it quite a lot.

That's okay. We all have our secret vices, our midnight tipples, our sweet indulgences. Writers buy books on 'how to write'. We wrap them in plain paper covers so people don't know our addiction.

Now we know what the problem is.

You've got a ton of characters—some you'd like to keep, some that seem a bit extraneous, and others that just claw their way back into your story regardless of how much you try to discard them.

What to do? Solutions please!

Maybe you could park a few in a file folder for the next book in the series? Maybe you could turn what started out as an intriguing supporting character into your next great protagonist, the star of their own show in another book?

Too many bad guys? Save one for another time. They have a long shelf-life and usually mature with age if kept in a dark place.

You consult your textbooks. And immediately you realise how inadequate you are. Who knew there were so many different *types* of characters? And they all sound so delicious. It's like sampling a box of chocolates. But you know if you gorge yourself on even more characters, bad things will happen. Unless you're the literary version of an Olympic triathlete, you'll never shed enough character calories to slim your story down.

All these fascinating types of characters supercharge your imagination. This creates a massive conundrum— how do you know which *type* of character would be best for your story? And how do you know how *many* characters you need?

You haven't solved your problem. Your addiction to textbooks about writing characters has only made it worse. In the end, you may begin to doubt you're good enough to write your own story. How can that be? Maybe you should hire someone else to do it for you. Boy, are you desperate.

I feel your pain.

Your characters don't seem to be measuring up to what the books are telling you they should be like. Just like an addict searching for their next fix, you hit the books again. You buy another textbook on characters to see if that one will give you the high you're looking for. These books on 'How to Write Characters' begin to consume you and fuel your doubts even further.

Giving up your search for answers is not an option. What to do? This is the problem: books on writing characters are great, they just don't answer two fundamental questions:

(1) What *kind* of characters does your story need?

(2) How *many* characters does your story need?

And then, the unimaginable happens—your mind goes to the movies again. It wants you to expand that first novel into a *series*, not just a sequel or a trilogy, a whole darn series! You've got it in your head there's more to your story than just the first novel. Your protagonist is an absolute adrenaline junkie; a glutton for punishment; an intergalactic Christopher Columbus.

Your head is pounding with ideas for your protagonist. New mysteries to solve. New killers to catch. New worlds to explore. New evil emperors to vanquish. Hercule Poirot, Jack Ryan, Harry Bosch, Luke Skywalker—if you follow these examples it will make your life miserable. Why? Because by creating a series, it means you're about to create a fictional *universe* and as we know, a universe of places and events needs a *universe of characters*. Your problem with characters just swallowed a whole bottle of steroids.

If only you had a tool that could simply and easily, without a lot of fuss, answer those two nagging questions:

(1) What *kind* of characters does your story need?

(2) How *many* characters does your story need?

Worry not.

That tool exists! It is The Character Quad.

CHAPTER TWO

Babies, Bathwater, and Textbooks

Let's time travel back to 1512, more than five hundred years ago, and plonk ourselves down in medieval Germany. Thomas Murner wrote a satirical book titled *Narrenbeschwörung*. Try saying that after a few beers in your local rathskeller!

A Google translation is *Fool Summoning*. I found a better translation: *Appeal to Fools*. You get the idea. Anyway, this old book contains a chapter titled, 'To Throw The Baby Out With The Bathwater'.

There are numerous scholarly explanations of what this phrase was referring to during medieval times but it's quite an achievement, after five centuries, thar this simple imagery has retained its original meaning without much alteration. Simply put, in your attempt to discard something of little value, don't mistakenly throw out the baby as well... or words to that effect.

The 'babies' here are your textbooks on 'How To Write Characters'.

In your quest for sanity, it's not time to throw these babies out. They have a place on your reference shelf for sure. Please indulge me as I talk about the four I bought and why I keep topping up their bathwater even though I wish I could drown a few.

The first one is *45 Master Characters (Mythic Models for Creating Original Characters)* by Victoria Lynn Schmidt. The book describes the meaning and literary use of archetypes. Archetypes have their origins in Greek mythology and got a modernised reboot in the 20th century through the efforts of Carl Jung, father of analytical psychology.

A dictionary definition of an archetype is:

Archetype—a primitive mental image inherited from the earliest human ancestors, and supposed to be present in the collective unconscious.

So far, so good?

In *45 Master Characters*, Schmidt describes 16 classic Greek archetypes (8 male, 8 female) each of which has a hero and villain version. This yields 32 total character profiles. The list is then expanded with the addition of a further 15 archetypes to cover supporting characters which results in a total of 45 master characters.

Schmidt then discusses the importance of knowing what your characters care about, what they fear, and what motivates them. With this understanding in hand, there are exercises to re-imagine how your plot would be affected if your protagonist or antagonist was changed from your initial choice to one of the other 32 main archetypes. In other words, it's possible to have up to 32 versions of your story, not including versions where you swap out one type of supporting character for another. You're encouraged to try as many combinations of male and female heroes and villains as possible before you die of writer's cramp.

What happens if your character is non-binary? Don't know. I don't have the latest edition. But simple math says there would be even more combinations.

45 Master Characters continues with a look at the masculine and feminine archetypal journeys. Characters aren't static cardboard cut-outs. They move. The long and short of it is... despite your best efforts, using your free-thinking, movie-inspired imagination to describe what makes your characters tick, this book says you might have 15 more options to consider for *each* character choice you've made. And that's for *each* gender. The odds are not in your favour. Your first attempt at selecting characters probably got it wrong.

It gets better.

In another one of my texts, *The Complete Writer's Guide to Heroes and Heroines* by Cowden, LaFever, and Viders, the authors are not satisfied with this seemingly simple approach.

First, they take the same 16 archetypes and give them new nicknames unrelated to their origins as Greek gods, just in case you memorised the first bunch (the literary version of the Microsoft operating system versus Apple's). They explain that each one of these 16 archetypes has 3 possible variations—core, evolving, and layered—giving 48 basic permutations of the original 16.

Not satisfied with that simplicity, they look at how each archetype interacts with another one. Opposites don't always attract. They describe 72 paired-interactions in each of 3 more situations—how they clash, how they mesh, and how they change—giving 216 different permutations of two characters interacting with each other. On top of that, the authors define the characteristics of 12 ensembles or groups consisting of more than two character archetypes. To help you understand these groups, they named them after famous films like *Ghostbusters* and *Saving Private Ryan.* That helps, doesn't it?

What are the odds you've been able to fit your character choice into one of these 216 archetype profiles without the latest artificial intelligence program helping you? If I was a gambling man, I'd say the odds of getting it right the first time are close to zero. You've got a lot of thinking to do. My recommendation: put your book on hold for about a year—maybe two. This will give you time to try each of the 216 permutations at least once. Come on, you can do it!

These textbooks graciously provide worksheets—what self-help book doesn't? I gave up. To this day, I couldn't tell you what archetypes I've used for my characters even if a gun was put to my head or someone offered me a million dollars.

I'm not disparaging any of these books or deterring you from buying them. I still have them on my reference shelf because there are nuggets of wisdom in them and who doesn't like a treasure hunt? I'm sure there are writers out there with photographic memories who would be ecstatic to upload 216 permutations into their brains. It's like memorising the dictionary. People win spelling bees with that technique all the time.

I want something I can easily remember. I don't want to be forced to reference my dog-eared notes on writing characters based on archetypes every time I put pen to paper. (Paper? That's how old I am. Forgive me. It just doesn't sound right saying, 'put finger to keyboard').

A more useful book is *Dynamic Characters: How To Create Personalities That Keep Readers Captivated* by Nancy Kress. Her books are terrific, easy to read, and helpful. She's a go-to mentor for all kinds of advice on writing.

In *Dynamic Characters*, Kress chooses a different route to get from A to B. She talks about how to make characters believable, how to characterise them through dialogue, the use of conflict and point of view, how characters interact with plot, and a host of other valuable nuggets of wisdom, gleaned from a career of very successful authorship.

However, she still doesn't answers those two niggling questions: what kind of characters should you have and how many? For what *kind* are needed, she defers to: *See texts above, bring abacus.* For the second part, *how many*, she doesn't say, so I guess you're still on your own.

The last book in this mini-review is *Characters and Viewpoint* by Orson Scott Card, part of the Writer's Digest series on *Elements of Fiction Writing*.

I've found this to be another down-to-earth book. It covers a lot of similar ground to Kress' *Dynamic Characters* and has useful chapters on how to raise the emotional stakes, creating voice and managing narrative, and the purpose of minor characters and walk-ons. At least I can *remember* what his points were, which is a prerequisite for a guide book isn't it?

Want to expand your library with books on 'How To Write Characters'? There are lots to choose from, beyond the four I've mentioned. Who am I to throw the baby out with the bathwater? Especially if it's your baby and your bath tub. So, I say, go for it. If that baby/bathwater axiom has stood for five hundred years, who am I to argue with its validity? Keep the baby (textbooks on characters) in the bath tub (your library), just in case.

I keep circling back to this—not one of these books have answers to the two key questions:

1) What *kind* of characters does your story need?

2) How *many* characters does your story need?

I've come to the conclusion that their overriding assumption is—you can figure out the answer to those two questions yourself. But once you've done that on your own, you're welcome to come back to classify your characters into one of the 45-character profiles—or if that's not enough choice for you, then one of the 216 permutations.

Got it. Thanks a bunch! I'll dust off my abacus.

The other possible reference source you can consult is the good old Worldwide Web.

So, I googled: *How many characters should a novel have?* Try it yourself. You'll find lots of blog posts and copious chat forums where this question is asked and some kind of answer is put forward.

I'll save you some time.

What are typical answers you'll find?

> *"It depends on your story, genre, and reader expectations."*
>
> *"The answer is simple but not definitive. I would say that it depends."*
>
> *"There are no rules in writing."*

Yes, these are real quotes from real posts answering the question, *How many characters should a novel have?*

Really? Oh boy, that was super helpful.

Okay, don't throw the baby out with the bathwater just yet! How about this idea? Wait until that baby grows up, send him/her to college to get their MFA in creative writing, and maybe by then, they'll bring home a *new* textbook which gives the answers you're been looking for. What are the odds of that?

No worries. Just kidding. You don't have to wait that long. Keep reading. You hold the answer to your questions in your hands right now.

CHAPTER THREE

The Hero's Journey and The Big Bang

A common recommendation whenever any expert offers advice on how to write characters is—whatever your plot involves, authors need to send their characters on a Hero's Journey.

This isn't a guidebook on the Hero's Journey and a single chapter isn't enough to do justice to the topic. But I'm not going to deviate from that sage advice. Why? Because knowing what a Hero's Journey is, and how to use it when constructing a story, is fundamental to the craft of creative writing—so fundamental in fact, that if you're reading this guide, I'm going to take a giant leap of faith and assume you already know what a Hero's Journey is.

So, all I'm going to do is give some brief perspective to lay the groundwork for how The Character Quad can help with your Hero's Journey.

The godfather of the Hero's Journey is Joseph Campbell. His Wikipedia entry starts:

"Joseph John Campbell (b. 1904 – d. 1987) was an American writer... and a professor of literature at Sarah Lawrence College who worked in comparative mythology and comparative religion. His work covers many aspects of the human experience.

Campbell's best-known work is his book The Hero with a Thousand Faces (1949), in which he discusses his theory of the journey of the archetypal hero shared by world mythologies, termed the monomyth.

Since the publication of The Hero with a Thousand Faces, Campbell's theories have been applied by a wide variety of modern writers and artists... He gained recognition in Hollywood when George Lucas credited Campbell's work as influencing his Star Wars saga."

George Lucas credited Campbell with influencing *Star Wars*? Whoa—that got my attention!

Turns out Campbell took Carl Jung's archetypes and expanded that idea like the Big Bang Theory.

I encourage you to put 'Joseph Campbell' into Wikipedia's search engine and read his biography. Then seek out his books, or find one that explains in depth how his Hero's Journey can be applied to creative writing.

Or just google the words 'Hero's Journey'. When I did, I got 215,000,000 search results. Yes, really—215 million results! That's influential by a million orders of magnitude.

In many ways, if an author doesn't believe in the concept of the Hero's Journey it's like a person disavowing the laws of gravity. Sorry, but it's impossible to wake up, believe Newton's theories aren't true, and then float around the room on willpower alone. You could do that if you live on the International Space Station. But we don't.

The Hero's Journey, like the law of gravity, is so fundamental to creative writing, it's annoying. I can't watch a movie or a TV show without a thought bubble bursting out of my head that says, "Aha! See that? That's the *Refusal of the Call...* or... They're *Approaching the Inmost Cave.* They'd better watch their steps!"

In some cases, it's so obvious what the scriptwriter is doing, it's comical. But audiences lap it up. They return to their screens time and time again to watch movie sequels, or the next series of a TV show, to follow the protagonist yet again, as they take up a new Hero's Journey.

Why? Because Carl Jung was right; because Joseph Campbell was right. And begrudgingly, I have to admit— because those textbooks on archetypes are right.

The magnetism of the Hero's Journey works. Humankind does indeed have a collective unconscious. We love to identify with heroes and watch them vanquish villains. The baby is playing in the bathwater, giggling away, splashing in our face, and saying in babyspeak, "Don't fool with the Hero's Journey, bro. You want to float? Jump in. The water's warm."

This brings me to the infamous 'plotter versus pantser' duel at dawn. When I first started writing I was asked which one—plotter or pantser—I was. I had no idea what a 'pantser' was.

Someone explained that a pantser was a writer that just started writing 'by the seat of their pants' and let the story take over the narrative as if by magic. The assumption is the pantser's story will unfold organically while it's being written. This flow of creative consciousness will ultimately lead to some resolution.

The theory is, your characters will come to life in front of your eyes as you write and that somehow, as if by magic, the story will be told by *them*—not you—as long as you keep on writing. You follow where your characters want you to go, not the other way around.

Stephen King is a proud pantser. But he's writing mostly in the horror genre, carefully building his premise and characters as he writes, and then letting the story unfold.

But there are many genres that rely on setting out the plot in advance, at least in outline form. Simple paper index cards work. It's not complicated. Scrivener automates this.

For me, plotting the story beforehand has a myriad of useful purposes. My first novel was a mystery thriller. When you write a mystery, the 'big reveal' is usually at the end. How on earth could you construct a mystery without plotting it out first? Where would you hide the clues, the red herrings? You need some kind of structured sequence of events to do that, right?

Same with a thriller. Your protagonist may know a serial killer is on the loose but the good guy hasn't caught him/her yet. To make a thriller interesting, the author creates a 'ticking bomb' literary device, puts obstacles in the way of catching the bad guy, more victims die along the way, and the killer threatens the good guy within an inch of his life. How would you organise all that in a sensible way if you're writing by the seat of your pants?

One purpose of plotting is often overlooked. In the very *act* of plotting, the need for certain kinds of characters becomes obvious. Just when you think you've pre-planned your list of characters, a plot 'hole' emerges and you realise you need a character to help fill it.

Not all characters in a story are introduced upfront to the reader all at once. They pop in and out depending on their *role* in the plot. But if you don't start with a framework for the plot, how will they pop up as you write? What *role* do they play?

Oops—their roles? What roles? You never told me about roles!

Well, I kinda did. Because it's the answer to the question:

(1) What *kind* of characters does my story need?

Wait a second—that's a question, not an answer!

True. But that's why I plot out my stories in advance and don't *pants* them (is that even a verb?). When I plot out a story, I know what *kind* of characters I need. Same thing with question (2) How *many* characters does my story need? By plotting the story in advance and assigning characters to a role in that plot, I can approximate how many characters I need. It doesn't limit me from adding more if I find a need for them.

I organise all this by using a tool I call The Character Quad. The key to The Character Quad is simplicity.

The objective I had when I invented it was to find a tool that's easy to remember. That's easy to use. That's intuitive, no PhD required. A tool that's easy to construct once you've done it once before. And once you've created any Character Quad, a tool that's easy to refer back to as you write, without needing a refresher course that interrupts your muse, or without having to look up complicated assembly instructions in some literary operation manual. 215 permutations, anyone?

The last thing you want to do is stop writing because you've forgotten what The Character Quad is trying to tell you. And the very last thing you want is to re-read the gibberish in this guide book again.

Trust me, once you've been taught The Character Quad, you won't forget it.

Using a tool like The Character Quad can even help those who have a preference to write freestyle. By creating a Character Quad before you begin writing, it can help you see what might be missing in the story—either in terms of the number and kind of characters, their roles, or their journeys.

Ready to take the first step?

Okay, but I need to make sure you and I are on the same page with the meaning of two words.

What the hell... really?

It's just two words. Honestly, just two. I promise. No more than that. But they're important.

CHAPTER FOUR

Defining Power & Wisdom

The two words are: Power and Wisdom. They form the two axes of The Character Quad.

Let's create The Character Quad.

Create an expandable Two X Two table like this in your word processor or in writing software (like Scrivener):

I use Scrivener because I create my plots using its electronic index card feature. Scrivener is a wonderful authoring tool and I highly recommend it. It's tricky to learn because it's so sophisticated. It has so many features. I'm continuously discovering new ones. The best thing about Scrivener is that after you create your Character Quad, you can store it in Scrivener's Character folder. You can retrieve it quickly with a single click. No need to jump from one doc file to another, just navigate between sections in a single Scrivener file that contains all your manuscript chapters, character profiles, and research.

Okay, that Character Quad we just created looks totally naked. What do I do next?

Label the axes of your Character Quad like this:

The Horizontal Axis is Power.
The Vertical Axis is Wisdom.
Each axis has two quadrants, High and Low.

The Character Quad is now taking shape. In the future you won't need the arrows or even the labels because as soon as you begin using the Character Quad you'll see how easy the labels are to remember.

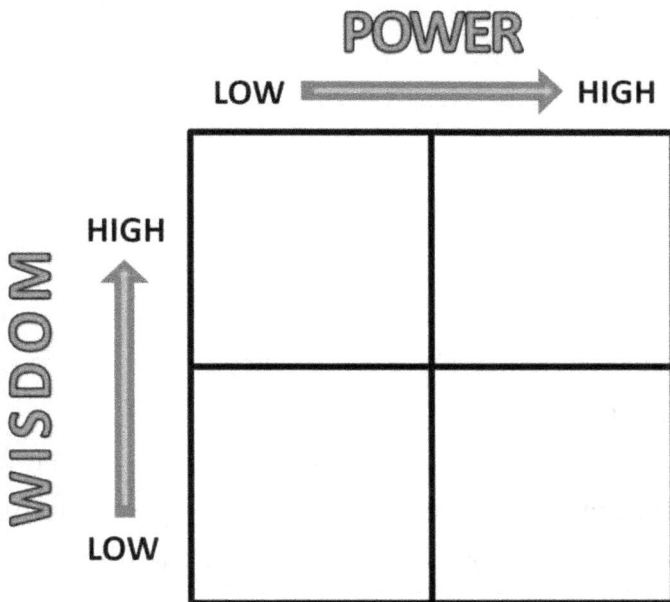

POWER

LOW ➡ HIGH

HIGH

WISDOM

LOW

Okay, so far, so good. Not hard, was it? I told you creating The Character Quad would be simple.

You've now created four distinct quadrants that are unique combinations of Power and Wisdom:

Lower Left:	*Low Wisdom / Low Power*
Upper Left:	*High Wisdom / Low Power*
Lower Right:	*Low Wisdom / High Power*
Upper Right:	*High Wisdom / High Power*

We're going to define the terms Power and Wisdom with special meanings specifically designed for authors who are writing characters.

These words—Power and Wisdom—are such common terms it's easy to arrive with preconceived notions about their definitions.

Don't worry, I'm not going to stray too far from what dictionaries say they mean. But it's important to realise each of these terms will take on a *special meaning* in the context of your story and more specifically, as they apply to the characters you put in it.

POWER in this case relates to your character's position of authority and control in the world you're building.

Similarly, *WISDOM* relates to the knowledge and insight they've acquired within the system of societal norms and structures you've created.

What may be powerful and wise in a thriller may take on a different dimension in a space opera or a magical fantasy. The point is: you're building your universe with its unique rules and boundaries; you are the one deciding what limits you want to place on your character's abilities, whatever they may be.

The concept of a quad diagram with High/Low sections like this is not new. Businesses use quad diagrams for problem solving and strategic planning all the time. A typical one might place Competition and Co-operation on the two axes. It's usually more common to have opposite meanings on each axis which makes The Character Quad unique.

How you label the axes depends on the purpose for creating any kind of quad diagram. The purpose for our quad diagram is clear—to compare character roles in the writing of fiction.

How we define what is meant by Power and Wisdom in the context of character roles is the foundation of everything going forward. If you need to come back and re-read anything, this next section with those definitions is it.

POWER = AUTHORITY + CONTROL

Power comes from *both* authority and control.

The most powerful characters in a story often are the ones that create the rules and are instrumental in administering them. However, authority doesn't always come from having a superior position at the top of some kind of hierarchy. Authority and control can be exercised by anyone, not just those with lofty titles who issue orders to subordinates. The most powerful characters in your story are those with the ability to control events regardless of their social or organisational status.

For example, mothers and fathers have been given de facto authority over their children by our social and legal conventions but anyone who has children knows that doesn't automatically confer control. How parents establish control comes from their use of psychology—how they create a reward/punishment system to establish control over their children's behaviour.

As we construct The Character Quad, you will need to think of power—authority and control—in more subtle ways and in more *relative* terms.

Powerful characters in your story often gain their authority over others not be commanding them but by manipulating them or coercing them—knowing *what to do* and *how to do it* is important, which means control also comes from the use of superior knowledge as we'll discuss next.

WISDOM = KNOWLEDGE + INSIGHT

Wisdom comes from both knowledge and insight.

Intelligent people or people who have acquired a high degree of knowledge can very often be extremely naive because they lack some critical insight—they haven't learned how to navigate 'the system' they live in.

On the other hand, someone with low knowledge isn't necessarily an idiot. Insight is a survival skill. Even the poorly educated have some level of insight. It's the issue of 'street smarts' versus 'book smarts'.

In your story, characters face risks they can't cope with because they initially don't have the wisdom that comes with learned experience. They can't foretell the danger that lay ahead because they might lack insight into what a danger in your world is, and what it isn't. An intelligent character can stumble into danger because they lack this insight.

Knowledge and insight have a very important dynamic. People are constantly learning something. We never stop learning. Your characters grow by acquiring knowledge from their learnings as the plot develops. Insight is then gained from experiences using that knowledge.

So that is why wisdom comes from a combination of these traits. As we will soon learn, the *relative* level of wisdom—the combination of knowledge and insight—will differentiate the characters in your story, both initially and as they grow through the plot.

So, what kind of character would occupy the very *extremes* of the Wisdom/Power Quad diagram?

LOW WISDOM / LOW POWER

If the extreme Lower Left quadrant represents Zero Wisdom / Zero Power, you would describe that character as a completely powerless idiot.

HIGH WISDOM / LOW POWER

If the extreme Upper Left quadrant represents ultimate High Wisdom / Zero Power, you would describe that character as being able to influence things by what they say but not by what they do, because they don't have any authority and can't control anything at all.

LOW WISDOM / HIGH POWER

If the extreme Lower Right quadrant represents Zero Wisdom / ultimate High Power, you would be describing a character as a totally bureaucratic robot, able to create mindless barriers simply because they've been empowered to do so but they don't have a clue *why* they're doing it.

HIGH WISDOM / HIGH POWER

If the extreme Upper Right quadrant represents the absolute Highest Wisdom / Highest Power, your character would be a god.

The truth is you don't want *any* of those four kinds of extreme character in your story. Not really. They aren't characters; they're cartoons. They're so extreme they're laughable. Their design flaws are so obvious they're comical. If the reader suspends belief in these characters—and they will, quickly—it's game over.

So, the magic of The Character Quad comes by placing characters inside one of these quadrants knowing they will never really reach the extreme points on a particular axis. Characters are much more nuanced than that. No one has zero wisdom. No one has ultimate power. These quadrants are *relative*. The quadrants operate on a sliding scale of *relative* value.

A character inside one of the low quadrants can have more wisdom than another one in that same quad. But both of them have less wisdom than the characters in the quads above them. See how that works?

A character may have less power than another but they are never truly powerless. Authority and control are relative and not static. Characters gain increments of power as they move through the story just as a character gains wisdom by experiencing events. Similarly, roadblocks arise that test the intellect of even your most knowledgeable characters. And power can be lost from the most powerful because they are not unconquerable, otherwise why tell the story? Readers want heroes to vanquish villains, or at least find the power to thwart them.

Now that we understand the concepts of *relative* Wisdom and *relative* Power, we're ready to give names to the types of characters you place in each of these quadrants.

These names are important because they help define the roles of the characters in your story and identify their relationships with each other.

Where textbooks describe characters in terms of *archetypes* and then educate us unmercifully on the many permutations that are possible from their personalities and motivations, The Character Quad helps us focus on just *four basic roles* derived from Power and Wisdom that *any* archetype can adopt.

Ultimately, The Character Quad can help you decide how many characters you need in your story. If you overload one quadrant, you have too many of one type, and at the other extreme, you shouldn't really leave any quadrant blank. We'll expand on these ideas going forward.

If you decide to kill off a character in a particular quadrant, at some point in your story, or in the next book in a series, you may want to find a character to take that place. The topic of whether to replace (or not) isn't a hard and fast rule. We'll discuss your options later if you decide *your* pen is truly mightier than *their* sword and you really want to bury that character six feet under.

We are now ready to label each of the four quadrants.

The Four Quadrant Roles are:
Underdogs, Mentors,
Overlords, and Underlings.

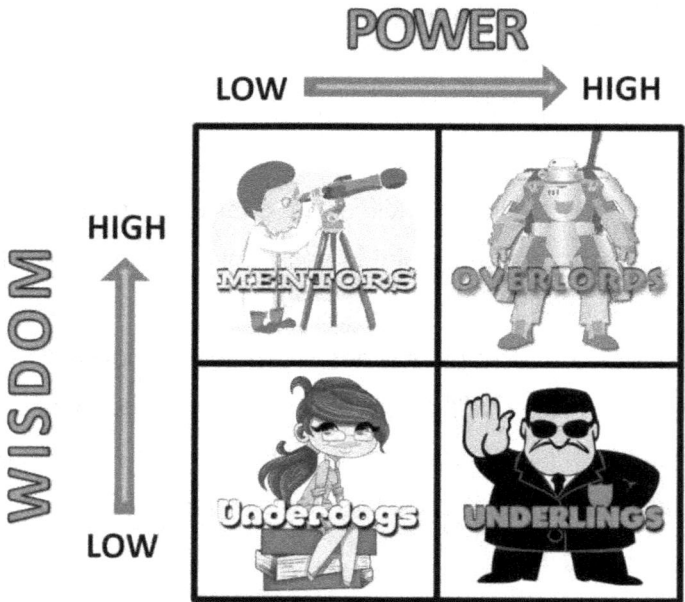

Summary: The Character Quad

The Character Quad is easy to construct:
    A Two X Two table.

The Character Quad is easy to remember:
    Two Axes—Wisdom and Power
    Two Levels—High and Low.

The quadrants form four roles:
    Underdogs, Mentors, Overlords, and Underlings.

Now that you know what it looks like, let's find out how easy The Character Quad is to *use*.

CHAPTER FIVE

The Character Quad - The Basics

I promised The Character Quad would be easy to construct and easy to use. I'm confident if you try it once—and hopefully find it useful enough to try again—you'll be able to create another Character Quad without referring to this guide.

They always say 'the devil is in the details'. That's certainly true when it comes to assigning your characters one of the four roles of The Character Quad. But again, these four roles are easy to remember.

A Word on Archetypes and
The Character Quad

The Character Quad is not overly complicated. It was designed to be as flexible as possible. In fact, I'm confident, if you are so inclined, you can chose any classical archetype for your character and place it into one of The Character Quad's four roles.

There's a deep psychological underpinning to these Greek / Jung / Campbell thingees called archetypes. It's undeniable. So, who am I to deny it? But I find them complex. People are complex and interesting characters should be complex—I agree with that. There are many possibilities when you create your character's personality and how that interacts with other characters. I get it. It's a reflection of the complex world we live in and the fantastic world you want to create.

But as I said, I rarely create my characters with a particular archetype in mind. Am I wrong in doing that? Don't know. I believe you can chose any one of the numerous archetypes to be the protagonist or antagonist in your story. If you're so inclined, do it. That's what I mean by not throwing the baby (archetypes) out with the bathwater. Those texts need to stay available.

The question is—do you have to use an archetype reference book to populate The Character Quad?

NO, absolutely not! Then it wouldn't be simple to use, would it? If you had a particular archetype in mind—it was the ideal type for your character—and you wanted to put that archetype into your story, can you use The Character Quad to assign them a role? YES, ABSOLUTELY!

Protagonists and Antagonists

Early on, we agreed it's impossible to write a story without any characters at all. I could be wrong about that. Please send me some feedback and an example if you think I'm wrong. I'd like to understand your argument.

Even something as abstract as a *setting* can be classified as a character.

Who is the antagonist in Andy Weir's *The Martian*? If his hero's journey is to safely get himself back home to Earth, who is stopping him? Yes, that's right. You've got it. The answer is the planet Mars. Everything he does is done by the planet's rules. The planet puts up environmental barriers; tests his intellect, fortitude and stamina; and it is his solution of finding a way to escape from Mars that makes our hero triumphant over his antagonist.

Here's another example of main characters without names. You don't have to give each member of an alien invasion army their own name. The terms Klingons or Romulans suffice. Of course, if you want to engage your protagonist with their leader, by all means give that particular alien a name.

In the movie *Cloverfield* nobody even uses a word as simple as 'creature' or 'monster' to describe the threat to the world. We don't know what it is, where it came from, or why it's doing what it's doing. But we sure as hell know why it's important to get out of its way. It's the antagonist. Our journey is to survive. It would have been nice to have given it a name like Godzilla or King Kong but if you want to use a placeholder for this character like 'The Creature' in your Character Quad, that's fine. The Quad will still work.

The common thread is that your story needs to have a protagonist (the mythical hero) and an antagonist. Even if you think you don't have an antagonist, there has to be something getting in the way of the hero on their journey. Planet Mars. The Klingons. The Creature. Identify it. Give it a name. Put it in the Quad.

Your protagonist(s) are UNDERDOGS.
Your antagonist(s) are OVERLORDS.

Note: you can have more than one protagonist or antagonist in your story. That's why I added the (s). For simplicity's sake, we're going to start the discussion as if there's just one of each kind. But you can have more.

Think Darth Vader and the evil Emperor, the co-antagonists of *Star Wars*.

We'll devote individual chapters to each of The Character Quad's four roles to expand what we mean. But since having a protagonist and an antagonist is so fundamental to every story, let's see why we've put them where they are in the Quad. This will help you understand the idea of 'relativity' between the four quadrants.

Your Protagonist is an Underdog. Always.

They inhabit the Low Power / Low Wisdom quadrant.

Let's face it, if they were the top dog in your story they wouldn't have much trouble reaching the goals they've set for themselves. They'd just decree it—like the phrase "so let it be written, so let it be done" (Pharaoh Ramses II in the 1956 film, *The Ten Commandments*).

"So let it be written, so let it be done" = I've accomplished my task, I've reached my goal, the journey is at an end. But if your protagonist can really do this at the very beginning, you don't have a story, do you?

Are Underdogs completely powerless? No. And they're not idiots either. They have skills they can use, maybe skills they don't even know they have. They will be tested and initially they may fail. But in terms of their *relative* Power in your story, they are lower in power than everyone else, except perhaps a sidekick or co-protagonist who are also co-Underdogs.

Your protagonist isn't dumb, but they lack either the essential knowledge or the critical insight to get what they want, perhaps both. Knowledge is learned. Insight is gained from experience by using that knowledge. This means an Underdog's *relative* Wisdom is lower than the characters in the other three quadrants.

Your Antagonist is an Overlord. Always.

They inhabit the High Power / High Wisdom quadrant, in fact they have the highest *relative* Power in your story.

They set the rules or can change them to suit their goals. They have control in critical areas of your world. It's hard to get around them. They have authority over not just Underlings but everyone else.

If they are criminals, they skirt official authority at will because they can. They have that knowledge. They have that control. Their authority may come with their position but it could also be subtle, derived from the influence they exert within your world.

Regardless, they get what they want from other characters by exerting their *relative* Power. At the start of your story, they have the most *relative* Power of any character. A serial killer on the loose can kill again. Darth Vader is building the Death Star.

An Overlord's *relative* Wisdom may come from specific knowledge that no one else possesses. That adds to their Power, even though other characters may have superior expertise in other areas. The point is, they've found a way to control even the more knowledgeable folks in your story.

Your antagonist's *relative* Wisdom is also high because of their insight—their ability to scheme, plot, evade, and manipulate the world as a result of knowing the 'ins and outs of the system', whatever that system of rules and authority is in your story.

We'll talk about the other two quadrants, Mentors and Underlings, in more detail in a later chapter but let me introduce them here so you know how they relate to your protagonist and antagonist.

Suffice it to say that a character with High Wisdom but Low Power is a Mentor.

This person usually mentors the protagonist, your Underdog. But they can also mentor the antagonist, your Overlord. They have superior *relative* Wisdom (knowledge and insight) than your Underdog. They may have superior *relative* Wisdom, from specific knowledge and insights that your antagonist, your Overlord, doesn't have. But in the latter case, Mentors don't have the same *relative* Power because they have less authority and control.

Similarly, Underlings have Low Wisdom but High Power and usually are under the control or influence of the Overlord. Their *relative* Power usually (but not always, we'll discuss later) comes from the control that is 'delegated' from a higher authority. This can be from within a defined hierarchy like the military or government, or a situational hierarchy like a work group or neighbourhood, or from society in general. Sometimes authority is left unspoken as is often the case within criminal organisations. Gang members know who controls what.

Can an Underling be of support to your Underdog? Probably not. Since Underlings have more *relative* Power than an Underdog, it's less likely an Underling would take orders or instructions from them without considerable resistance.

As far as *relative* Wisdom, Underlings aren't as wise as some of the other characters and that means they can come unstuck.

It would be easy to separate the four quadrants into two sections: the Protagonist's World of Underdogs and their Mentors; and the Antagonist's World of Overlords and their Underlings. But you will want to save some flexibility. These roles may not be fixed throughout the story. Remember the idea of crossing over to the dark side? Boundaries within The Character Quad can be jumped as the story progresses. We'll see how later.

Here is an illustration of what your Hero's Journey looks like when represented by The Character Quad:

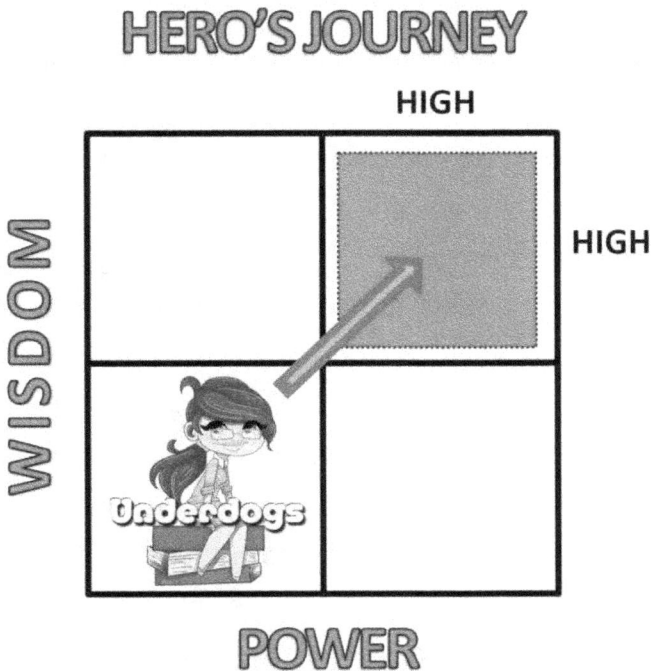

Managing how Underdogs and Overlords relate to each other is undoubtedly the most important relationship building aspect of your story.

To reach their goal, to complete their Hero's Journey, your protagonist, your Underdog, needs to gain both Wisdom and Power. Their goal by the end of the story is to finish up in the upper right quadrant, more powerful than they were at the start and wiser too.

Does that mean they will have superior *relative* Power over their antagonist at the end of the story?

Yes, it's possible but it doesn't have to be exclusively so. Let's explore this with some examples.

At the end of Agatha Christie's novels, Hercule Poirot reveals who the murderer is and has them arrested—exercising power over them. That's how the story might end but not how the story started.

By reputation, Hercule Poirot is a genius, with tremendous powers of deduction and reasoning so his knowledge and insight should be very high at the start of each story, right? Not really. His wisdom is relatively low because as each new case begins, he knows little or nothing at the start of his investigation. He is powerless to apprehend anyone because he hasn't established who the guilty party is. Poirot builds his knowledge by finding clues and gains insight by piecing the clues together until he reaches a point of higher relative Wisdom and Power over his suspect. He moves from the lower quadrant to the upper quadrant to complete his journey.

But it's equally possible the Underdog doesn't completely vanquish their adversary. Villains return in other stories.

In Sir Arthur Conan Doyle's *Sherlock Holmes* novels and short stories, Moriarty continues his criminal ways. Such is the nature of an ongoing nemesis. However, in any given novel, Sherlock Holmes does solve that particular crime. Similarly, James Bond and Spectre are examples of a hero with a repeated nemesis.

Your Underdog achieves a higher level of Power by removing the obstacles put in front of them in order to complete the *external* part of the Hero's Journey. But they also must resolve the *inner* Journey which is overcoming the limitations of their personality and character flaws. We'll get into that aspect of the Hero's Journey in our discussion on character arcs.

You can see from this simple visual representation of the Hero's Journey how a sequel or a novel series could arise if you wanted to expand your story universe.

At the end of Book One, your Overlord may live to see another day but has been diminished in Power. However, the Overlord can rise again by reclaiming their *relative* Power in Book Two and beyond.

In *Star Wars*, one Evil Emperor, the Supreme Dictator of the Galaxy, is vanquished but is replaced by another one in the next story. The nemesis to our Underdogs is an Evil Emperor regardless of name. Until the Empire or its derivatives are eradicated once and for all, there will always be another Hero's Journey for the *Star Wars* Underdogs to undertake.

In your story's sequel, your renewed Overlord (or a completely new one) is placed in the upper right quadrant of The Character Quad. Your Underdog's *relative* Wisdom and Power again starts at a new low in relation to this new adversary and they confront dangers they have not yet learned to overcome. Yes, they have more skills, and new learnings from their previous experiences, but once again, they need to apply them. This is exactly what *relative* Wisdom and *relative* Power mean. Let the next Journey commence!

CHAPTER SIX

The Character Quad - Wizard of Oz

Our first example of constructing a Character Quad will use the characters from *The Wizard of* Oz. I'll refer to the storyline from the 1939 film based on the 1900 novel, *The Wonderful Wizard of Oz* by L Frank Baum.

Let's remind ourselves of The Character Quad's four roles and their relationship to Wisdom and Power:

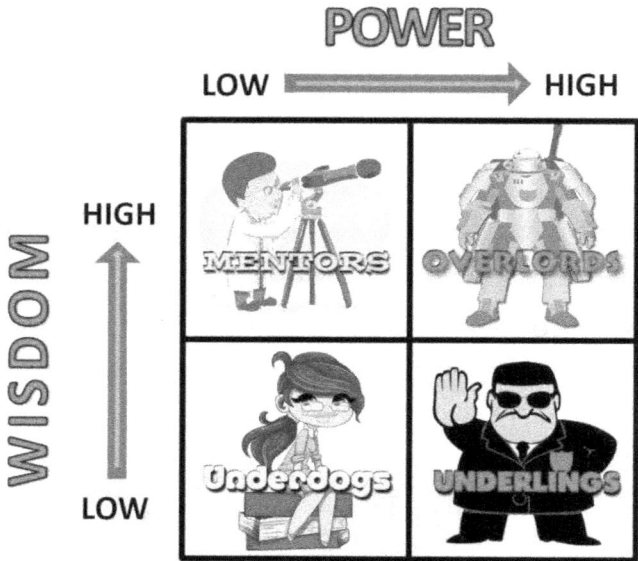

In discussing the *Wizard of Oz* example that follows, we're going to dispense with the labels on the axes and the High/Low arrows. By all means, continue to use these axes labels when you construct your own Character Quads. I'm confident you'll soon remember which quadrant is which by the end of this guide—Underdogs go on the lower left, etc. You can eventually dispense with the axes labels if you want too as well.

Let's get started. Once we've dispensed with the Oz cartoons in our discussion, we'll add the four quadrant names and populate them with a finalized list of characters in each one so you'll see what a finished Character Quad looks like when you do one yourself.

The Wizard of Oz is so famous, let's get right to the heart of the story by naming the primary protagonist and antagonist:

Our Underdog is Dorothy.
Our Overlord is the Wicked Witch of the West.

Dorothy's quest is to get back home to Kansas. The Wicked Witch wants revenge on Dorothy for killing her sister and absconding with the ruby slippers. The Wicked Witch stands in the way of Dorothy reaching her goal of getting home. Events escalate. The Wicked Witch kidnaps Dorothy's dog Toto and Dorothy must vanquish the Witch to get him back. Dorothy then needs to find a way to get from Oz to Kansas. Enter the Wizard of Oz.

The antagonist, the Wicked Witch of the West, has the highest *relative* Power in the story through her magic and she has the highest *relative* Wisdom too. The Wicked Witch can see everything that's going on in Oz through her crystal ball. That's a great metaphor for insight isn't it? In most stories, the antagonist has some way of doing this without the use of magic but it's a great visual representation of what we mean by insight.

Dorothy is clearly the Underdog. She's less powerful than the Witch and must gain *relative* Power throughout the story to counteract the Witch's threats and also gain *relative* Wisdom to find a way home.

Dorothy hasn't a clue about the weird land of Oz. She's been magically plopped down into Oz by the tornado so she's pretty low on the Wisdom scale. Dorothy needs to gain Wisdom in order to navigate her way around. One way of doing that is to get a Mentor. Dorothy needs help. She needs to know what to do and where to go.

Enter The Good Witch, Glinda. The Good Witch is her Mentor. We know which quadrant to put her in, don't we?

The Good Witch's Power is limited. That's clever, isn't it? If a character can simply help the protagonist overcome the antagonist with a wave of a magic wand, there wouldn't be a story.

The Good Witch can't vanquish the Wicked Witch, that's not how things work in the Land of Oz. But she can advise Dorothy on how to get home. The Good Witch gives our Underdog the ruby slippers. She tells Dorothy about the Wizard of Oz and shows her the way to the Yellow Brick Road. The Mentor has given Dorothy some much needed *knowledge* and *insight* into Oz, its weird landscape, and people. After that, it's up to Dorothy to find her way around. Dorothy's *relative* Wisdom is now growing.

Dorothy needs more Power to propel herself back to Kansas but the Good Witch isn't going to hand that Power to her on a plate. The Mentor's *relative* Wisdom is high but her *relative* Power is not much greater than Dorothy's.

This doesn't have to be the case with every Mentor in your writing but in this story it was the author's choice. The Mentor's power in *The Wizard of Oz* isn't as great as the Overlord's. Therefore, in *relative* terms, The Good Witch has less Power than the Wicked Witch. Glinda, the Good Witch fits neatly into the upper left quadrant of High *relative* Wisdom / Low *relative* Power—the Mentor quadrant.

Enter Dorothy's three companions...the Tin Man, the Scarecrow, and the Cowardly Lion. What role do they play?

There's only one primary protagonist in this story and that's Dorothy. Her new companions are major characters but in secondary roles. What quadrant do they go in? We're going to put them in the Underdogs quadrant with her: Let's understand why.

Why are they Underdogs? Well, clearly they don't have much Power. After all, The Tin Man has been rusted shut for goodness knows how long. They have their own problems to solve and lack the intellectual wherewithal (Wisdom) to solve them.

Once they decide to help Dorothy on her Journey, it becomes clear they also have Hero's Journeys of their own...to find a heart, find a brain, and find courage.

They have a common nemesis in the Wicked Witch who tries to set the Scarecrow on fire. And when Dorothy suggests the Wizard's magic might help them get to their goals, their secondary Journeys interlink with her primary one in a common purpose and destination.

Which leads us to the Wizard of Oz.

You've guessed it... he's an Underling:

Why is the Wizard an Underling?

He doesn't report directly to the Overlord, the Wicked Witch, does he? No, but that's not always necessary as we said before. It has to do with the concept of *relative* Power and *relative* Wisdom.

It appears at first he's a real wizard but that's the art of the conman. He uses all kinds of pyrotechnics and projected images to make himself look more important and more powerful than he actually is—aren't most bureaucrats like this? The Wizard has used this *relative* Power to bluff his way into owning his own castle complete with an entourage of guards and the admiration of the local Oz-folk. So, in *The Wizard of Oz*, he has more *relative* Power than our Underdogs.

As far as *relative* Wisdom goes, they discover he doesn't know any more about how to get back to Kansas than our Underdogs do. In the end, the Wizard is exposed as a total fraud. The Wizard turns out to be a pretty benign character behind all that bluster but before we find that out, he uses his conman-derived Power to throw a major monkey-wrench into the story by demanding Dorothy fetch the Wicked Witch's broomstick as a condition to give her his help. Typical bureaucrat. Creates roadblocks. Lots of control. But acts a bit mindlessly.

Minor Characters
To Quad or Not to Quad?
That is the question.

There are many other characters in *The Wizard of Oz* beyond the major ones. Just because they have minor roles doesn't mean they should be ignored.

We need to assign these minor characters to one of the four roles in our Character Quad. This essential step addresses the issue of whether you have too many characters in your story or not enough. If you don't put these minor characters in your Character Quad, you won't know that answer.

There's another important reason to document minor characters this way. If you're planning to write a series, you will inevitably need to expand your character universe in subsequent stories. Of course, you can invent new characters but don't overlook the opportunity to re-use a minor character in one story as a major one in another. We'll dig deeper into that angle in another chapter.

So, what minor characters in *The Wizard of Oz* have we left out of the Character Quad so far?

In The Land of Oz:

Toto

The Mayor of Munchkinland

The mayor's assistant, the Coroner

The Lollipop Guild (three munchkins)

The Munchkin townsfolk

Nikko, The Leader of the Flying Monkeys

The Flying Monkeys

The Wizard's Guards

The Oz-folk

The Angry Apple Tree

Back in Kansas:

Uncle Henry and Aunt Em

Professor Marvel (the Kansas Wizard)

Almira Gulch (the Kansas Witch)

The Kansas Farmhands—Hunk, Zeke, and Hickory

Bet you didn't realise there were so many characters in *The Wizard of Oz*!

This is what happens with characters. They pop up everywhere. Each one has a purpose. Each one should have a role.

It's time to define a new category—The Bit Character.

Bit Characters

In *Characters and Viewpoint*, Orson Scott Card describes bit characters as walk-ons and placeholders. This kind of character is just a part of the scenery, part of the 'milieu'.

Very often they are never named. They perform a simple task or participate in an event. Examples in your writing might be a concierge at a hotel desk, a booking sergeant at the police station, protesters at a rally, etc.

In The Character Quad, you should place these kinds of bit characters in a simple list just below the Quad diagram.

This is not just a score-keeping exercise, especially if you've named a bit character. It's quite possible you may want their role to grow in other novels of your series. You might 'promote' them into a role that fits inside one of the quadrants in further novels. But for now, bit characters like this *don't* occupy one of the four key roles in the Quad and should just be catalogued below it for reference.

Take note: be careful not to mis-classify a character as a bit character when they're not. My rule of thumb: use the Hero's Journey as a guide.

If a character plays an active and continuous role in another's character's Journey, they have a minor role in the story and should be classified as a minor character.

If their role is so minor their absence in the story would leave the Hero's Journey unaffected, then they're truly a part of the background scenery and are simply a bit character.

Let's test this question... minor character or bit character?... with our list of miscellaneous characters from *The Wizard of Oz*:

Toto—a bit character. Nothing would essentially change if the dog wasn't there. He's a plot device to set Dorothy up on her fateful Journey and give the Witch something to steal. You could argue he's a co-Underdog with her. I could go either way if you twisted my arm. My argument is—he's not really on a Journey of his own, he'd follow her anywhere. If the witch had stolen something else that was treasured by Dorothy—something she desperately wanted back like a family photograph or a necklace—would that object become a minor character? No, it wouldn't. So, why should the dog?

The Mayor of Munchkinland—a Mentor. Surprised? He's maybe a minor one, but he does advises her about the Yellow Brick Road, the first piece of knowledge given to her about navigating the magical land of Oz. He also has more relative authority than Dorothy by virtue of his high station in Oz.

The mayor's assistant, the Coroner—a bit character. He pronounces the Wicked Witch of the East dead when it's obvious she is (a house fell on her) so his role isn't really essential to the story. This knowledge doesn't advise Dorothy. His role is to just step out of the background, make his pronouncement, and step back. Classic bit character. Nothing would change if he wasn't even in the story. Ding, dong, the Wicked Witch is dead. Everyone can see that without him.

The Lollipop Guild (three munchkins)—bit characters. They sing a song in the movie to welcome Dorothy to Munchkinland but if the movie version wasn't a musical, they wouldn't be needed.

The Munchkin townsfolk—bit characters. The definition of 'milieu', part of the scenery.

Nikko, The Leader of the Flying Monkeys—an Underling. Finally, we get that personification of the evil-doer following orders! His part is small but his actions are significant to the story. We'll put him in the Underling quadrant and label him as a minor character. Who knows, maybe after the Wicked Witch is vanquished, Nikko could rise to the station of Overlord as a major character in a future novel, *Dorothy and the Evil Flying Monkeys*.

The Flying Monkeys—bit characters. Again, a nice visual part of the background scenery. But it's Nikko who snatches Toto and brings him back to the Witch. The other flying monkeys are just his escort squadron.

The Wizard's Guards—bit characters. Apart from marching around, they do nothing. Dorothy gets in to see the Wizard regardless. They are just there for colour and dramatic effect.

The Oz-folk—bit characters. More of the munchkin-like 'milieu' of Oz.

The Angry Apple Tree—bit character. Cute but no cigar. Maybe if the Angry Apple Tree had done more to interfere with Dorothy's Journey, we could elevate this denizen of the forest to a minor antagonist.

Uncle Henry and Aunt Em—Mentors. They are the reason Dorothy wants to return home. They are the loved ones in her life who are wise and protective. Their roles are minor but significant to the Hero's Journey.

Professor Marvel (the Kansas Wizard)—bit character. Warns Dorothy of the tornado but anyone who grows up in Kansas should know by now what one looks like and what to do if you see one coming. She would have fled to safety without him.

Almira Gulch (the Kansas Witch)—Overlord. Yes, really. A minor one, but definitely the source of initial anguish in Dorothy's life as Gulch gets a court order to euthanize Toto for biting her. Sets up the Journey at the heart of the story. Definitely antagonist material even if just a minor role.

The Kansas Farmhands—Hunk, Zeke, and Hickory— bit characters. As Kansas counterparts to her Oz companions, they really don't have much of a role to play in her Journey. If they weren't in the story, that wouldn't have affected the plot. They simply acted as inspirations for her Oz companions but that's all they were.

Here's the Character Quad for *The Wizard of Oz*:

MENTORS:	OVERLORDS:
Glinda, The Good Witch	The Wicked Witch
The Mayor of Munchkinland*	Almira Gulch*
Uncle Henry*	
Aunt Em*	
UNDERDOGS:	UNDERLINGS:
Dorothy	The Wizard of Oz
The Tin Man	Nikko, The Flying Monkey*
The Scarecrow	
The Cowardly Lion	

* denotes Minor Characters

Bit Characters:

Toto, Dorothy's dog

The mayor's assistant, the Coroner

The Lollipop Guild and the Munchkin townsfolk

The Flying Monkeys

The Wizard's Guards and the Oz-folk

The Angry Apple Tree

Professor Marvel (the Kansas Wizard)

The Kansas Farmhands—Hunk, Zeke, and Hickory

As you can see from the finished Character Quad for *The Wizard of Oz*, there's a good balance of the four roles, and a good balance of both major and minor characters. If you want to asterisk the minor characters you could (as I've shown).

The difference between major and minor is very subjective. If your Character Quad contains a long character list in one particular quadrant, it helps to assign major/minor designations to make sure you've got the balance right between the quadrants.

Which leads us to the next question: what would happen to the story if one of these quadrants was entirely blank?

It would definitely shine a spotlight on the main battle between the protagonist and the antagonist. The story narrative would narrow its focus. You might want to do this in your story. It's your choice. It's your story. We'll discuss a reason *not* to do this later on.

How might eliminating characters and their roles affect this particular story, *The Wizard of Oz*? The Wicked Witch would have to do her own kidnapping. Dorothy would have to buy a guidebook to Oz.

You can see from this simple example of a Character Quad that not only do other characters add colour but through their *relative* Power and *relative* Wisdom, their interactions with other characters add drama. We'll get into more detail on using the Quad to identify character interactions in the chapter on *Conflict*.

In the example of *The Wizard of Oz*, we didn't need to reference a textbook and select one of 216 permutations of archetypes. We didn't need a three-dimensional abacus or an astronomical chart of the night sky to construct our Character Quad.

It was easy, right?

CHAPTER SEVEN

The Quad's Law of Relativity

When we first defined Power and Wisdom we discussed the *relative* nature of both when comparing a character in one quadrant of The Character Quad (say a Mentor) to a character in another (say an Underdog). We discussed the idea that placing characters inside a quadrant will never really result in any character reaching the extreme points on either axis—Power or Wisdom. No one has zero Wisdom and no one has ultimate Power. Your characters are not cartoons.

We said the quadrants of The Character Quad operate on a 'sliding scale' of *relative* value. One character has more *relative* Wisdom than another. One has more *relative* Power.

We also made note that characters inside the same quadrant can still have *relative* differences between them.

When it comes to knowledge of the Land of Oz, Dorothy as an Underdog has less Wisdom than The Tin Man but both are still Underdogs in relation to other characters in the story and they are both protagonists.

Which leads us to an awkward question—do we need to *apportion* differences in Power and Wisdom between characters in the same quadrant? Do we need to define a character, like a Mentor, as one that occupies the upper half of the Mentor quadrant while another Mentor occupies the lower half? Is that really necessary? Is there any value in doing this?

If you said yes, then I would ask, why stop there? How about dividing each quadrant into thirds or quarters? Or how about using the metric scale to differentiate characters? Can we say a Mentor occupies the 7/10th position of Wisdom within the Mentor box in order to differentiate them from a character who's only at 3/10ths? Can we really be that precise?

NO... NO... the answers to all those questions are an emphatic NO.

Please don't do that.

I hope you agree, all of this sub-dividing would be absurd. It's also totally unnecessary.

If you have more than one Mentor in your story, you know the *relative* differences between them because you've created those differences. The fact that one is wiser on some subjects may also mean they are less wise on others.

The fact that an Underling has more bureaucratic power than another is understood by you when you write about them. In some situations, you may have decided that a particular Underling will have less Power than another Underling. So, what's the point in differentiating them to the *nth* degree when a *relative* judgement will suffice? It's not necessary to sub-divide your characters this way. It just complicates things.

Keep everything subjective. Think about your characters using simple *relative* comparisons. Things *change* as the story unfolds. Power and Wisdom will change in *relative* terms as well. Keep it simple. It's more or less, not inches or centimeters. The whole point of the Character Quad is to keep everything *simple*...simple to understand and simple to use. So, put your metal rulers away.

CHAPTER EIGHT

Underdogs

It's right to start our discussion of individual quadrants at a place where your characters will have the lowest *relative* Power and *relative* Wisdom—the quadrant known as the Underdogs.

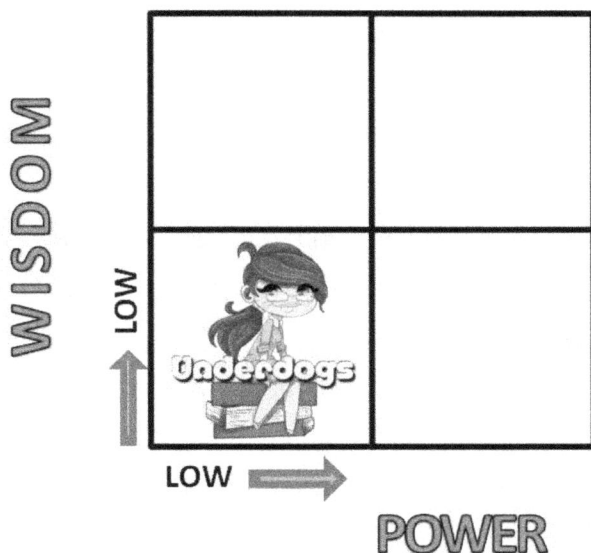

Without a doubt, your primary protagonist will occupy the Underdog quadrant at the beginning of your story.

Whatever choices you make, in whatever world you choose to create, the common thread for your Underdogs should be their low *relative* Power and *relative* Wisdom in that world. This will automatically force the question: what's in their makeup that's holding them back?

Low Power and Wisdom mark the classic starting point for the Hero's Journey; the beginning of most protagonists' character arcs. Being powerless and lacking wisdom at the start means the only way forward is up. The character must find the desire and means to do better. That is the essence of the Underdog's motivation at the beginning of your story.

Let me emphasise again, your chosen genre shouldn't matter when using the Character Quad.

When creating characters for your world, we can easily apply the Character Quad to whatever technology, society, economics, and politics you choose. The Character Quad will apply equally in historical novels whether set in Tudor England or in Civil War America, or in any historical era; to a future colony on a faraway planet or to a fantasy kingdom of elves; to murders in a big city or in a small town—the genre and setting don't matter.

Power is a combination of authority and control. We would expect our Underdog to feel—at least initially— quite powerless in the world you're creating.

Consequently, an Underdog that feels powerless is probably struggling politically, socially, or economically. Show how your Underdog needs to face these challenges and confront any threats in order to survive and thrive in the world you've created. Show how your Underdog lacks the resources—economic, physical, or emotional—to overcome these barriers and obstacles, unless they are able to increase their Power or Wisdom, or both.

Are all Underdogs economically disadvantaged or politically oppressed? That's a common trope—an easy way to type-cast an Underdog. After all, many stereotypes fit nicely into the role of Underdog—from revolutionaries and peasants; to starving artists and the wrongly accused. By all means, pick one that fits. The list of stereotypes is quite large but it's important not to fall into the trap of thinking every Underdog must be downtrodden. Remember again, we are talking here about your Underdog's *relative* Power. Their lack of Power needs to be placed in context—it is *relatively* low compared to others in the story, but it's not zero.

For example, a character in the aristocratic world of 18th century France may be low in the social pecking order within the King's Court but outside the court they are still an affluent and powerful person compared to the great unwashed—the poor unfortunates who have to eat cake if there is no bread. Given the right circumstances, even a rich person can start off in your world as an Underdog with lower Power and Wisdom *relative* to your other main characters.

Similarly, a detective hunting a serial killer is an Underdog, not because they're poor, but because they start off with low Wisdom—they lack the knowledge that finding evidence will give them and lack the insight to understand the killer's motive. Without this Wisdom, they lack the Power to apprehend. The world will continue to be at the mercy of the serial killer until the detective gains the Power and Wisdom to stop the evil-doer from killing again.

Every genre has Underdogs that start out with low *relative* Power and *relative* Wisdom.

In your sci-fi world, a commander of a planetary defence force is your Underdog because they are initially pitted against superior alien technology. Until they gain the knowledge and power to counteract it, the aliens will hold the upper hand.

In your epic fantasy, your Underdog starts a quest without a clear map of where to go and what dangerous monsters lurk inside your world's caves along the way. They lack knowledge and insight as they start their quest; their *relative* Wisdom is low. They also lack authority and control over the means to get there; their *relative* Power is low.

In general, Underdogs strive to gain a better standing in life but may not know how to achieve that. Perhaps your Underdog lacks self-confidence, is riddled with self-doubt, and is an under-achiever. Underdogs are often wanderers, free spirits, dreamers; shunned by others, outcast, and inwardly focused.

Much has been made of the 'flawed' character as an Underdog—a big trend in genre literature and in particular in television series. In these cases, the Underdog is going through some kind of personal crisis whether it's from a divorce, alcoholism, drug addiction, or mental health issues. It's hard to object when a writer chooses a character with these problems because personal crises like these are real and pervasive in society. We can't ignore that reality.

Authors should try to reflect the diversity of the world in their stories. But character flaws should not be used simply as devices to gain sympathy for your characters— that would be a kind of voyeurism. They should truly reflect the Hero's Journey—both external and internal. Your character's *inner* Journey is often set in motion by the choices you make about your character's backstory.

Defining your characters' imperfections is a tricky process that requires a lot of thought. Can The Character Quad help? Yes, by using The Character Quad's concept of low *relative* Power and low *relative* Wisdom.

When you're developing an Underdog's backstory, ask yourself the question—what Power does my Underdog need to reach their goals? What Power has my Underdog lost and what prevents them from getting it back? What knowledge and insight—Wisdom—does my Underdog need to acquire as they proceed on their Hero's Journey?

For example, if you want your character be flawed, rather than focusing the reader on the effects of their alcoholism—a scene where your Underdog is drunk and embarrasses themselves—focus on the reasons they got drunk in the first place and how their alcoholism has caused a loss of *relative* Power in their lives. Define success as getting that Power back. And then show the reader the barrier to success alcoholism has created and the personal challenges the Underdog must overcome. That's the best way of creating sympathy for your Underdog. You want the reader to root for your Underdog. Show them how your Underdog increases Wisdom and gains Power as the story unfolds.

You can see from this discussion how the concepts of low *relative* Power and low *relative* Wisdom apply in creating your Underdog. There are many possibilities and opportunities for the type of character you create here. Don't be limited by conventional thinking or by stereotypes.

CHAPTER NINE

Overlords

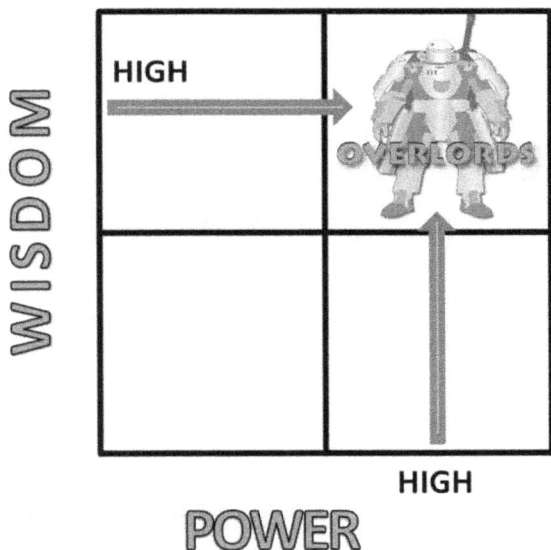

The quadrant known as the Overlords contain characters with the highest *relative* Power and highest *relative* Wisdom. There may be more than one Overlord, but generally they are all considered to be antagonists.

"Each film is only as good as its villain. Since the heroes and the gimmicks tend to repeat from film to film, only a great villain can transform a good try into a triumph." —the late, great film critic Roger Ebert.

There is usually a primary antagonist in opposition to your Underdog Hero (the primary protagonist). This Overlord stands in the way of your Underdog Hero's goals.

This Overlord is often shared with other characters in the Underdog quadrant. An example of this is the Wicked Witch of the West in *The Wizard of Oz* who is both an antagonist to Dorothy and also to her sidekicks.

It's possible to have multiple antagonists, each one being the Overlord to different Underdogs. Overlords can also have antagonistic roles with characters other than Underdogs such as with Mentors and Underlings. Give these other antagonists names and put them into the Overlord quad too.

In defining an Overlord, let's get the obvious out of the way. An Overlord is the major source of threats, roadblocks, and barriers thrown down as impediments to the Hero's Journey. They do this by using their superior *relative* Power—their authority and control.

These threats can be physical—threats of bodily harm to our Underdog hero such as direct combat, incarceration, impending execution. Or they can be circumstantial—the Overlord creates events that hinder the hero's progress. Threats can be psychological— actions that make the Underdog feel impotent or fearful. Threats can be directly expressed (physical, circumstantial) or implied (psychological).

Whatever manner of threat or challenge the Overlord lays down, the common thread in all of them is the Overlord exercising their superior *relative* Power to thwart the Underdog.

Overlords stand in opposition to your protagonists by directly commanding resources against them or by manipulating other characters to do their bidding. The purpose of either tactic is to maintain control and ensure the Overlord's continued dominance. Overlords are able to do that by exerting the authority you give them. That authority may come from their social status in the community or family; a high political position like Supreme Leader; a military or police rank; business executives with corporate titles; being the head of a criminal gang; or a host of other official roles that signify a position of authority and control over others.

But Overlords also exert other means of control that don't require organisation charts to define them.

The concepts of high *relative* Power and high *relative* Wisdom mean Overlords can also rule through their psychological dominance alone.

An example is the elderly patriarch or matriarch in a family, a character who has no official 'title' but dominates other family members by exerting the Power and Wisdom given to them by virtue of their position in the family hierarchy. Fear of defying the patriarch's wishes for example could be enough to exert control over your less powerful Underdog.

Another example is a work group of relatively equal colleagues where your Overlord has Machiavellian or narcissistic tendencies that make life difficult for your Underdog. These traits manifest themselves in the Overlord's obsessive need to be the top dog in every situation even if they have no formal position of authority.

When we think of the kinds of antagonist an Overlord can be, we often default to the usual stereotypes— authoritarian rulers like dictators, kings, or queens. Bullies and gangsters fit the bill, as well as malevolent bosses. We then assign traits based on stereotypes, like egomaniacs or megalomaniacs, highly self-confident individuals that lack compassion and are excellent at scheming.

Yes, your Overlords can be any of these things, that's true. But I would encourage you to research other psychological profiles. By reading up on the classifications of mental disorders for example, you may find an intriguing psychological underpinning for your Overlord's traits. There are plenty of personality disorders to choose from. This will help create Overlords with more complex flawed personalities.

Sociopaths make great Overlords. Books have been written on how easily sociopaths have climbed the corporate ladder in real world businesses. Their lack of empathy and remorse makes them good cost-cutters and ruthless with people. If you want more on this topic, especially if you're a crime writer, I highly recommend *Snakes in Suits: Understanding and Surviving the Psychopaths in Your Office* by Dr Paul Babiak and Dr Robert D. Hare.

Sociopaths and psychopaths make excellent Overlords because their motivations don't simply come from exercising official authority but are derived from their need to maintain control over others in all kinds of evil ways. There's no point in killing a mouse as soon as you catch one, the cat says, when you can spend all day playing with them.

It's true that Overlords are generally malevolent characters. As antagonists, they are often referred to as villains (I think the term Overlord is a broader umbrella as we will discuss soon).

Villains have archetypes that come from mythological origins. Fairy tales and myths are crammed with villains getting in the way of the Hero's Journey.

Vanquishing a villain terrorising your world may be the goal of your Underdogs. But by recognising the Character Quad's emphasis on *relative* Power and *relative* Wisdom, the end point of your Hero's Journey can be written with more subtlety than just having the Overlord die by the sword.

Yes, dragons need to be slayed but if you have a novel series, that means creating a new monster or adversary for the next novel.

The Character Quad encourages you to find ways to have your Underdog gain more *relative* Power and *relative* Wisdom throughout the story so they can be equal to, or even superior to your Overlord as their Hero's Journey is resolved but don't overlook the opportunity to carry over that particular Overlord into another novel.

How? Find ways for your Overlord to gain back their superior Power and Wisdom in the next novel.

In *Star Wars*, it takes a long time to vanquish Darth Vader for good. He's a truly delicious villain. He may be thwarted when the Death Star is destroyed but Darth Vader re-emerges in another episode with even more dastardly world-destroying technology and aren't we glad he did?

Here's a question for you—is there such a thing as a benevolent, Underdog-friendly Overlord who is also an antagonist?

The answer is... yes!

A prime example comes from Norse mythology. These myths have been adapted into the Marvel Super-Hero Universe. We are, of course, talking about Thor and his relationship to his father Odin.

Norse myths place Odin at the pinnacle of their hierarchy of gods. He is the patriarch whose rule is unquestioned and whose role is unassailable. However, Odin is often opposed to what his son Thor wants to do— especially when it comes to cavorting with those pesky mortals. Thor challenges Odin's authority and in return Odin either puts obstacles in Thor's way or doesn't come to his aid when Thor gets into trouble. In this way, Odin tries to teach his wayward son a lesson.

Odin is an Overlord but he is not the principal antagonist in Thor's adventures. That role often goes to his mischievous and malevolent brother Loki, or to some other god-like entity that disturbs the order of the universe or threatens Earth. However, if you were to construct a Character Quad based on Norse mythology, Odin would fit in the Overlord quadrant.

Can you think of other Underdog-friendly antagonists? I'm sure you can. If not...make one up in your own story!

There's a third type of Overlord to consider. This type of Overlord can be referred to as a 'non-personal' antagonist.

Huh? A what?

Yes, an antagonist may not always be a person. In some stories, your primary antagonist may be a force.

Say that again?

Consider a volcanic eruption that threatens to destroy a city, or an asteroid on a collision course with Earth. In these cases, the Overlord with the most *relative* Power is not one of your named characters. But it is definitely a force that creates the biggest threats and obstacles in the way of your protagonist's goals, which likely include saving his hide and the hides of his loved ones.

The setting of the novel itself can be the antagonist. In Andy Weir's *The Martian* there are no individuals that stand in the way of the Underdog. The astronaut is trapped on Mars, alone and abandoned, with no obvious way of getting home. He fights all kinds of adversities and creates all kinds of plans—some of which end in mini-disasters—in order to escape the planet. The planet itself throws down the biggest obstacles—sandstorms, food scarcity, lack of oxygen, distance to home and its safety.

You guessed it, the planet Mars is the antagonist. It is an Overlord. Its *relative* Power is considered supreme until the Underdog turns his ideas into physical ways to get rescued. In his character arc, our astronaut Underdog's unrelenting determination results in achieving the Power to defeat the planet's hold on him.

Society itself may be the antagonist—through its restrictions on personal freedom or other rules of oppression. Dystopian and post-apocalyptic science fiction is full of these kinds of non-personal antagonists, ideas that usually relate to society's collapse or overbearing technology.

In the case of *The Hunger Games* by Suzanne Collins, society's rules force citizens into life-and-death competitions. The Games themselves are the Overlord in addition to the evil people who run them.

In George Orwell's *1984*, Big Brother is not a human character in the traditional sense but an idea that represents the impact of authoritarian rule on society. Through Big Brother, society creates explicit threats whenever an Underdog attempts to stray from the rules to increase their personal freedom.

Big Brother watches everything and controls everyone, even with the implied threat that Big Brother is monitoring your thoughts. Big Brother is in every way an Overlord and can be put in that quadrant.

When we discuss Conflict in a later chapter, we'll expand on these concepts of the 'non-personal' antagonist. In the mean-time, if you want to place a non-personal antagonist inside the quadrant of an Overlord, give it a name, and by all means do so!

CHAPTER TEN

Mentors

We've discussed the two quadrants with the most extreme relative values of Power and Wisdom. Now it's time to talk about the other two. We'll start with Mentors, characters with high *relative* Wisdom but low *relative* Power.

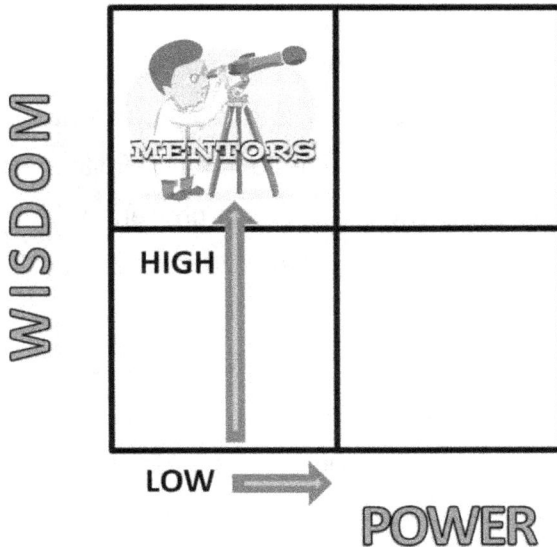

In relative terms, Mentors have greater Wisdom—knowledge and insight—than Underdogs and Underlings. Whether their Wisdom is greater than your Overlord's is up to you. The choice you make with the latter will determine how much help you want your Mentor to be. Nevertheless, Mentors share a relatively low Power profile in the story and will be at the mercy of the Overlord's superiority in that regard.

We often say the 'pen is mightier than the sword' and 'knowledge is power'—so what gives? Why doesn't this apply? Shouldn't a Mentor have some kind of knowledge-based Power?

Yes and no. It has to do with our definition of Power as a combination of authority and control.

The Mentor quadrant is positioned to have relatively less Power because Mentors by definition don't have sufficient authority or control to challenge the Overlord's supremacy, at least initially when the Hero's Journey begins.

By definition, Mentors have even less power than Underlings. There are many sources of authority and control and mindless bureaucrats can throw obstacles in front of Mentors as well, given an Underling's higher *relative* Power.

Mentors are not completely powerless, no character is. How they use their Wisdom to gain advantage is certainly an example of flexing their intellectual muscles. And definitely, a Mentor's Wisdom will give them the intellectual ability to overcome obstacles as they arise, even when put there by Underlings.

So, who are these Mentors in your story and what purpose do they serve?

First, let's deal with the knowledge part of Wisdom.

Beyond a doubt, Mentors possess superior knowledge in areas that matter to your Underdogs. This can be scientific or political. It can be social or spiritual. Their knowledge helps other characters analyse threats and develop options to counter them. Mentors propose plans and strategies. When we add superior insight to their knowledge, we get characters that have a big-picture view that other characters lack. This is a desirable asset when trying to plan the way forward and develop ways to overcome roadblocks and obstacles. Mentors can be strategically and politically astute or even psychic. In short, they know what to do because they've seen it before, perhaps in more ways than one.

Mentors can be very self-confident and assertive by virtue of their superior expertise and experience. On the other hand, they could be introverted; shy and withdrawn—they have expertise but it needs to be drawn out. The fact that Mentors have high *relative* levels of knowledge and insight doesn't necessarily mean they are all extroverts. An interesting choice to make, isn't it? These personality types are opposites but either would work for a Mentor.

Mentors can display strong analytical abilities and self-discipline, can be more data-driven than emotional, and because of that, may perhaps be a bit socially awkward, to the point of either being detached, obnoxious, or effete.

Again, there are many choices of character traits you can use to define a Mentor as long as you recognise their high *relative* Wisdom when assigning their role in the story.

Mentors are relatively low in authority and control on the Power scale.

This could be a causal reason for their timidity. They can even be recluses—the stereotypical solitary wise man or woman living in a cave that the Underdog stumbles across. That's basically how Luke Skywalker came across Obi-Wan Kenobi in *Star Wars*. Maybe your Mentor is only confident within their own circle of colleagues and lacks confidence within the broader power structure outside them.

You can choose to give your Mentor a low or a high status within your world's official hierarchy of titles. There are many choices you can make as you position your Mentor in relation to the other characters.

How would a timid, low-level recluse with amazing savant-like coding skills assist your Underdog? What happens when this Mentor comes face-to-face with the Overlord in the story? Does your Mentor fight or flee?

In general, Mentors are guides and advisers to others. They are someone's close confidante—not necessarily with the primary protagonist, maybe someone else? Again, choices to be made. In our example from *The Wizard of Oz*, the Good Witch is very much a guardian angel to Dorothy, and this trope is perhaps a too-obvious stereotype for a Mentor. But the Good Witch is definitely one.

Mentors can pursue a number of occupations where intellect is valued—scientists, engineers, doctors, lawyers, senior police officials and forensic investigators, etc. Science, engineering, and technology offer whole encyclopaedias of possible occupations a Mentor can have.

In the spiritual field, they can be religious leaders, prophets, life coaches, gurus, tribal elders, or shamans. In the supernatural realm, they can be wizards, sorcerers, psychic seers, fortune-tellers, mystics, angels, or spirit guides.

Having said all this, Mentors don't have to have a 'mentoring' occupation as such. Their role is to provide guidance through their superior knowledge and insight. This higher level of Wisdom produces admiration and respect from the other characters in your story regardless of whether that knowledge represents an occupation.

Mentors exist within family structures, businesses, or other types of social groups and organisations without the need to have a degree on the wall or a title on the door.

Don't forget the value of the insight portion of high Wisdom. Mentors can be street-wise members of a particular community with valuable insights on how to survive—whether that's in a poor urban neighbourhood or in the alleys of some cyberpunk metropolis. The ability to navigate around obstacles in any kind of society, to anticipate and avoid threats, to develop battle plans and strategies—all come from superior insight as well as superior knowledge.

Mentors can also provide guidance to your antagonists—that's right, to your Overlords!

Who says a Mentor's motives always have to promote good? But a word of caution—be careful not to confuse a Mentor with an Underling. We'll talk about Underlings in the next chapter and you'll understand what I mean.

Always position your Mentors to have superior *relative* Wisdom—superior knowledge and insight—than your Underlings possess. That defines the difference between a Mentor and an Underling.

Mentors are not always completely aligned with the goals of the Underdog's Journey. They can act with ulterior motives or provide a foil to the Underdog's lack of knowledge and insight. They can toy with the Underdog from a loftier position of Wisdom. Can you think of a character like this?

How about Dr Hannibal Lechter in Thomas Harris' *Silence of the Lambs*? Hannibal Lechter acts as a Mentor to FBI detective Clarice Starling in her quest to apprehend a serial killer dubbed Buffalo Bill. Compared to Clarice Starling, Lechter possesses a superior level of knowledge about the 'how-to' of murder—after all, he is a killer too. And he has superior insight—he was a skilled forensic psychiatrist. However, throughout most of the story, he is locked up in a maximum-security prison for the criminally insane. Ding, ding! His *relative* Power is even less than Starling's who has the freedom to act without being constrained by a jail cell.

Lechter toys with Clarice from behind his Plexiglas screen and revels in giving her mind riddles to solve. His sociopathic brain knows what it's doing. He leads her—gives her guidance—to the evidence she seeks and prompts her with questions she must answer to solve his riddles. A manipulative Mentor to be sure, but a Mentor nevertheless.

So, to be clear, Hannibal Lechter's position in the Character Quad of *The Silence of the Lambs* is not as an Underling (where higher control = more Power) or that of an Overlord (superior in both Power and Wisdom). He is definitely a Mentor, just not a particularly 'good' one in the moralistic sense.

Let's consider the character Gollum in *The Hobbit* and *The Lord of the Rings* by JRR Tolkien.

In the novels, the creature Gollum is torn between his lust for the Ring and his desire to be free of it. Bilbo Baggins finds the Ring in *The Hobbit* and passes it on to Frodo Baggins in *The Lord of the Rings*. Gollum relentlessly pursues the Ring, which he calls 'his precious', from one novel to the next until he falls into the fires of a volcano, where both he and the Ring are destroyed.

In Tolkien's stories, Gollum had superior Wisdom to Bilbo and Frodo Baggins. He knew a lot of things they didn't. He could navigate through all kinds of danger. He had insights they didn't have. And he used this superior Wisdom to manipulate them on their journeys through Mordor.

He certainly wasn't the primary antagonist and he wasn't on a par with the Power commanded by the primary Overlords.

His gift of guidance to the Underdogs was self-serving in the extreme. Gollum is described by literary critics as an evil guide, in contrast to the wizard Gandalf, a good guide. However, Gollum still fits the definition of a Mentor in our Character Quad even though he has ulterior motives in opposition to the Underdogs' goals. In this regard, his relationship with the protagonist Frodo Baggins was pseudo-antagonistic.

The examples of Hannibal Lechter and Gollum should give you inspiration to explore different ways to craft your Mentors. You have a lot of freedom with this; lots of choices.

Exploit this quadrant to create characters with interesting combinations of high *relative* Wisdom and low *relative* Power.

Have fun!

CHAPTER ELEVEN

Underlings

I have a confession. I love Underlings.

Of all the quadrants in The Character Quad, my imagination is drawn to writing Underlings as if it has been captured by some cosmic force of creative magnetism.

Underlings exhibit low *relative* Wisdom but high *relative* Power, and that particular combination is intriguing to me when developing characters. The trope of the mindless bureaucrat comes immediately to mind but this category has a whole host of possibilities for generating character-based chaos and conflict.

An Underling usually doesn't have the highest Power when compared to other antagonistic characters in your novel, that's true. But that's what makes them special in my mind.

I dispute the idea all Underlings are minor characters and they always need to be subservient to Overlords. Their command of a relatively high degree of authority and control can make them more than just supportive characters if you set your mind to it. Underlings can be pretty significant players in your story if you want them to be. Let's explore how.

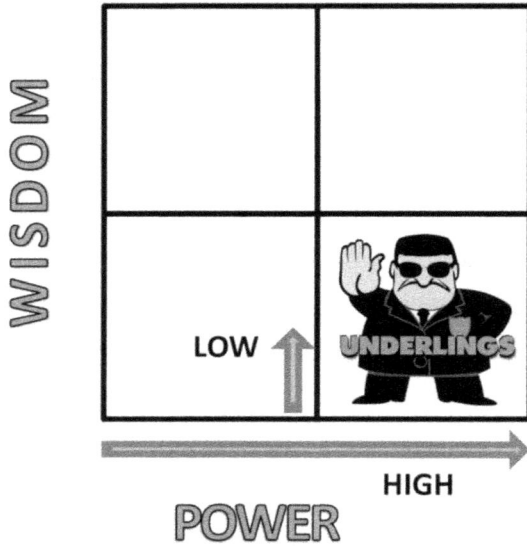

My all-time favourite Underlings in literature come from Douglas Adams' *The Hitchhiker's Guide to the Galaxy*.

What Douglas Adams has been able to do—with absolute comic brilliance—is take mindless bureaucrats and supercharge them so they jump right off the page.

I'm of course referring to the Vogons, his fictional alien race who are responsible for the destruction of the Earth as part of an intergalactic highway construction project to create a hyperspace express route.

I mean really, that sums it up nicely, doesn't it?

Our special planet—with its flawed but adorable human species and other unique flora and fauna—is just some unimportant blip standing in the way of mindless galactic-government bureaucrats whose main purpose in the continuum of space and time is to blast obstacles as big as planets from existence without any regard whatsoever. They are just following orders.

They are the perfect Underlings. The idea that someone whose trope involves creating obstacles decides an entire planet is actually an obstacle to be removed is a literary tour-de-force.

Douglas Adams describes the Vogons as slug-like and green-skinned, vaguely humanoid and bloated, and collectively "one of the most unpleasant races in the galaxy—not actually evil, but bad-tempered, bureaucratic, officious and callous".

They have "as much sex appeal as a road accident" as well as being the authors of "the third worst poetry in the universe". I love that last bit, don't you? I mean bureaucrats who write dull poetry? That's poetic justice, isn't it?

Douglas Adams nails it. When the movie came out, the Vogons appear in *The Hitchhiker's Guide* as larger-than-life cartoon-like personifications of what extreme Underlings might look like. I can watch the film over and over just for the pleasure of revisiting the scenes with the

Vogons—they are truly priceless expressions of what Underlings could be.

The idea of combining high authority with low wisdom creates all manner of opportunities to create characters from the standard tropes of bureaucrats, technocrats, and sycophants. Underlings populate professions like civil servants, low-ranking military and police officers, local politicians, and personal assistants to more powerful people.

The common denominator is their ability to create roadblocks and obstacles; and police rules, regulations, and policies with little regard to what might seem like common sense.

Control is everything to an Underling. They love to tamper in ways that will interfere with the Hero's Journey.

Underlings are generally methodical in their approach, task-focused versus people-focused, officious, pedantic and obsessive.

Underlings can be the consummate bullies, hired hit men, Mafia soldiers. They manipulate and harass other characters using the high *relative* Power they're given, either from their official position in an organisation, their unofficial position in a social group, or from the authority delegated to them by an Overlord.

They are rigid, not only in their actions, but in their thoughts. Underlings may be envious of those with knowledge; bewitched by those in higher authority; and unable to see their own faults. This latter personality flaw generates a degree of insecurity in an Underling that they overcome by exerting authority and control in ways that bolster their egos.

Sociopaths make great Underlings. They lack empathy, revel in their ability to control others, and act without regard to any consequences that might result. Again, I would refer you to the classification of mental disorders for guidance on sociopathic traits as well as to other obsessive-compulsive behaviours and anti-social personality disorders that you could manifest in your Underling.

They admire Overlords and may aspire to be one someday. This is a fantastic opportunity—why I love having a good Underling to nurture. Your current novel's Underling may be an Overlord-in-Waiting.

In this instance, their character arc would involve your Underling acquiring more experience and insight to raise their *relative* level of Wisdom. Early on, they may feature in an apprentice-like role in your stories.

Given more time to gain more *relative* Wisdom and by obtaining even more authority and control—more *relative* Power—you can grow your apprentice Underling into your next big antagonist Overlord.

Having a character in one novel as an Underling breeds familiarity with their character arc. Subsequent stories can advance that arc to one of an Overlord. Reward your readers with this promotional opportunity. It worked for Anakin Skywalker in *Star Wars*. He progressed from Underdog to Underling as he crossed over to the dark side, eventually reaching Overlord status when he became Darth Vader. If it worked for *Star Wars*, make it work for you too.

Inject some chaos into your stories with the clever use of an Underling.

CHAPTER TWELVE

Character Arcs and The Quad

In previous chapters, we discussed character archetypes and introduced how important the Hero's Journey is to constructing a story. There's another aspect of character building and development that every writer should master—the character arc.

We've mentioned character arcs in passing, in our discussion of the roles within individual quadrants. The assumption has been that you knew what was meant by a character arc.

How does The Character Quad fit with the concept of the character arc?

Let's find out.

Character arcs 'map' the progress of characters as characters change or 'grow' throughout the story. A character's progress inevitably means changes will occur to their *relative* Power and *relative* Wisdom.

Your characters will gain experience which means they gain Wisdom. They will overcome obstacles and learn new skills which increases their Power. Their *relative* position within a quadrant will change and their *relative* Power and *relative* Wisdom when compared to everyone else will change as well.

How much your characters change—and whether that's enough to reach their goals—is the topic of this chapter. Only *you* can decide how your characters have gained or lost Power and/or Wisdom by the end of the story. Again, these changes are *relative* to where everyone started.

Just like we discussed in the topic of archetypes, The Character Quad supplements but does not replace the concept of the character arc. And certainly, it would take another whole book's worth of explanation—possibly more than one—to explain the character arc and its importance. This has already been done by other authors in ways better than I can describe.

This guide is not going to be sufficient to deep-dive the topic of character arcs so I defer to the superior expertise of others on this topic and encourage you to find an in-depth guide of your liking. But to get you started, I'm going to refer to my go-to reference—KM Weiland's *Creating Character Arcs: The Masterful Author's Guide to Uniting Story Structure, Plot, and Character Development.*

KM Weiland is a very successful author of historical and speculative fiction who has also written a host of excellent guides on the craft of writing. Her blog posts are worth reading. She provides a continuous stream of excellent free guidance on a whole range of writing-related topics. In *Creating Character Arcs*, she states, "The character drives the plot, and the plot moulds the character's arc. They cannot work independently." That's a pretty profound statement. We ignore that at our peril.

So, what is a character arc?

From Wikipedia: 'A character arc is the transformation or inner journey of a character over the course of a story... The character begins as one sort of person and gradually transforms into a different sort of person in response to changing developments in the story. Since the change is often substantive and leading from one personality trait to a diametrically opposite trait (for example, from greed to benevolence), the geometric term *arc* is often used to describe the sweeping change. In most stories, lead characters and protagonists are the characters most likely to experience character arcs, although lesser characters often change as well.

A driving element of the plots of many stories is that the main character seems initially unable to overcome opposing forces, possibly because they lack skills or knowledge or resources or friends. To overcome such

112

obstacles, the main character must change, possibly by learning new skills, to arrive at a higher sense of self-awareness or capability. Main characters can achieve such self-awareness by interacting with their environment, by enlisting the help of mentors, by changing their viewpoint, or by some other method.'

The key word in all of this is...*change*.

Characters *change*.

They change in response to events, in response to their environment, and in response to obstacles and conflicts. Since conflict is such an important topic in its own right, we will expand on this in an upcoming chapter.

The key point here, as stated by KM Weiland in *Creating Character Arcs,* is:

The main character seems initially unable to overcome opposing forces, possibly because they lack skills or knowledge or resources or friends.

Well, we've learned all about knowledge as we've constructed The Character Quad. In fact, we've gone one step further by combining knowledge with insight to create Wisdom, one of our principal axes.

To overcome such obstacles, the main character must change by learning new skills and arrive at a higher sense of self-awareness or capability. The Character Quad helps you identify this exact kind of growth..

Learning new skills means increasing their *relative* level of Wisdom. Achieving a higher sense of awareness or capability will result in an increase in their *relative* level of Power. More Power—more authority and control— means our characters are more capable of removing obstacles and achieving their goals.

So, The Character Quad is completely in sync with the idea of the character arc.

Let's examine the lowest quadrant in The Character Quad to illustrate this:

The Character Arc of the Underdog

Underdogs lack *relative* Wisdom and *relative* Power when compared to all the other characters in the other quadrants. Underdogs start from a position of deficit, a lack of critical abilities. They feel inadequate in response to their challenges.

In a literary sense, they have a black cloud following them. In a visual sense, it could be represented like this:

Our Underdogs don't stay under this black cloud forever. KM Weiland is right—the character drives the plot, and the plot moulds the character's arc. They are interdependent.

As the story progresses, this arc doesn't just go up and down like the flight of a cannonball but should be visualised as a continuous wheel of growth that cycles throughout the plot as the characters acquire small bits of Wisdom and Power along the way.

The plot is like a rolling wheel that leaves its imprint on our character like tire treads do on soft earth.

This process of continuous character growth can be visualised like this: **

As our character progresses through their Hero's Journey, whatever weaknesses and deficits they exhibited initially can be overcome by growing their knowledge and insight—their Wisdom—and by acquiring more authority and control—their Power.

This cycle of character growth doesn't just apply to your primary protagonist. It applies to all the Underdogs in your story as well as to all the other characters not in the most powerful quadrant (the one that contains your Overlord). If anything, the Overlord's *relative* Power diminishes during the plot as the other characters' *relative* Wisdom and Power increases.

Previously we said character arcs 'map' the progress of characters as they change throughout the story. You can use the Character Quad to visualise different routes for these character transformations. You can then write these 'routes' into your story by changing your characters' *relative* Wisdom and *relative* Power as the plot progresses.

Let's explore this simple way to visualise character arcs using the quadrants of The Character Quad.

**Footnote: Many thanks to John Hain for putting his outstanding illustrations into the public domain for everyone to use freely. You can connect with more of his work here: John Hain on Pixabay

We've discussed how the main route of character growth for the principal Underdog is reflected in a drive to achieve Power and Wisdom equal to or better than their antagonist, the Overlord. This character arc for an Underdog can be visually represented as:

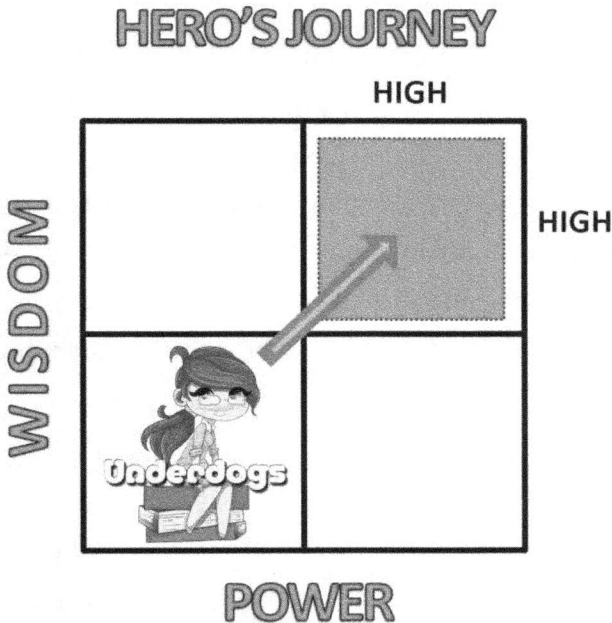

But what other 'routes' can we create to visualise character arcs?

The most common other routes for character transformation *within* a novel are:

(1) Underdog to Mentor

(2) Underling to Mentor

(3) Mentor to Overlord

(4) Underdog to Underling

(5) Underling to Overlord

In this discussion we'll try to keep it simple (that's the theme!) by talking in terms of a character arc represented by a transition from one Quad role to another.

However, there's nothing stopping you from using the Character Quad to create complicated character arcs involving several steps—from one role to another, followed by a transition to a third one, all within the same novel.

As long as you understand how to manage changes in *relative* Wisdom and *relative* Power as your characters move through the plot, there are many possible routes of character growth that can be visualised using The Character Quad.

To introduce the concept of using The Character Quad as a 'roadmap', we're going to focus on character arcs *within* a novel. But the Quad's real power comes from transitioning character roles from one novel to another in a series. You'll soon see how to create those great opportunities as we discuss our examples.

Underdog to Mentor

One way to perform an 'Underdog to Mentor' transition within a story is to choose an Underdog character—*not* the primary protagonist—and 'promote' them to Mentor by having them gain some valuable knowledge or insight that supports the primary Underdog on their Hero's Journey. This is a common character arc and relatively easy to create.

In *Star Wars*, Obi-Wan Kenobi starts his role as an Underdog by being an apprentice to Jedi master Qui-Gon Jinn. But as all *Star Wars* fans know, as Obi-Wan Kenobi increasingly masters the good side of the Force he becomes a principal Mentor to the young Anakin Skywalker and later to Luke Skywalker. His character arc starts with Underdog and ends with Mentor in one of the stories and then Obi-Wan Kenobi is positioned as a Mentor from that point forward in subsequent stories.

Important Note: It is unlikely your *primary* protagonist—your main Underdog character—would end their Hero's Journey as a Mentor. Why not?

The Hero's Journey progresses when the primary Underdog gains enough Power and Wisdom to complete their Journey and reach the level of the Overlord's quadrant.

In order for an 'Underdog to Mentor transition' involving the primary protagonist to occur in a single story, the primary Hero's Journey would have to be replaced by a secondary character's Journey.

How could that be done? Perhaps the first primary Underdog is side-lined and is forced to take up an advisory role. In this case, another Underdog must continue some kind of common Hero's Journey. To make this *primary* Underdog to Mentor transition work in your story would be very difficult.

Let's make up an example and see just how difficult this would be to write. Batman suffers a crippling injury and is forced to mentor Robin who now becomes the principal Underdog on the journey to defeat The Joker. Perhaps you could do this, but why would you want to?

This hypothetical example is all very *external* and plot-driven. This kind of transition fails a very critical test—the lack of personal growth in a character arc that's needed to resolve the *inner* journey of the primary protagonist.

Sidelining Batman to turn him into a Mentor after he's already been the primary protagonist is a complicated character arc to manage.

How would a relatively inactive Batman resolve his issues of personal growth from his hospital bed? It's not totally impossible I guess, but unlikely and certainly challenging to write.

This leads us to this important conclusion—the 'Underdog to Mentor' character arc is not a common one when it comes to the *primary* protagonist. The most common way to create this 'primary Underdog to Mentor' transition is to view it from the perspective of a novel series where the Mentor is an Underdog in the first novel and transitions to a Mentor in the sequel or subsequent books, as we saw with the character Obi-Wan Kenobi in *Star Wars*.

In Novel #1, the character arc of personal growth is
resolved when your primary Underdog prevails at the end
of that story. You can then assign that character the role
of Mentor at the beginning of Novel #2 to support a new
Underdog who begins a new Journey.

Underling to Mentor

How does this character arc happen? To understand
every case of character transition, we simply need to refer
to the *relative* positions of Power and Wisdom.

In order for an Underling to become a Mentor, two things must happen—they lose *relative* Power (authority and control) *and* they gain *relative* Wisdom (knowledge and insight).

Can you think of ways to grow your Underling into a Mentor?

The first step might be the loss of status—the Underling is stripped of their authority. Or perhaps your Underling decides they've had enough of being subservient to an Overlord and willingly abandons that role. In both cases, their *relative* Power is diminished.

At the same time, this must involve an Underling growing in *relative* Wisdom. You will need to show in your story how the experience of being an Underling has resulted in acquiring knowledge or insight that will be of benefit to other characters, especially the Underdogs.

In James Leo Herlihy's novel *Midnight Cowboy*, the naïve protagonist Joe Buck meets Rico "Ratso" Rizzo, a con man. Ratso is a ne'er-do-well petty criminal, an Underling that lacks high status in the criminal world but has greater Power than Joe by virtue of his experience. He befriends Joe but then cons him out of twenty dollars. After Joe confronts Ratso's treachery, they resolve their differences and begin a business relationship as hustlers. Ratso becomes Joe's Mentor.

Whether a newly-minted Mentor acts in the best interest of your Underdog or still serves their Overlord (but in a much-diminished position of authority) is a choice you would have to make as your plot unfolds. Your story's events will drive all of these changes.

Mentor to Overlord

To affect this character arc, the Mentor must gain more *relative* Power, like gaining the knowledge of the dark side of the Force in the *Star Wars* examples.

Instead of using their higher *relative* Wisdom to benefit the Underdog, the Mentor becomes an antagonist. This transformation can be written within a single story or can occur from novel to novel in a series.

As we have discussed previously, not all Mentors may be well-intentioned towards your protagonists. Some may be disguised as Mentors but are acting for the antagonist Overlord. They are essentially corrupt Mentors using their higher level of knowledge and insight to thwart the hero on their Journey.

At the end of the story, the Mentor-to-Overlord transition often occurs when the corrupt Mentor becomes the successor to the defeated Overlord. But there are others ways to write this.

George Orwell's classic dystopian novel *1984* contains one of the most famous examples of a Mentor becoming an Overlord by the end of the story.

In *1984*, the protagonist Winston Smith secretly opposes the totalitarian rule of Big Brother and toys with ideas of rebellion. Winston believes his superior, an Inner Party official named O'Brien, is part of an underground resistance. O'Brien invites Winston to his flat, gives him a banned book, and becomes Winston's Mentor. At the end of the novel O'Brien is revealed as having been an agent of the dreaded Thought Police all along and is in charge of Winston's torture and final subjugation.

1984 is a novel that truly breaks the mould. Our Underdog Hero does not prevail. In the end, the hidden Overlord O'Brien gains Power over our poor protagonist and the regime of Big Brother is the victor.

Underdog to Underling

In popular culture, this character arc is said to occur when a protagonist 'crosses over to the dark side'.

In George Lucas' *Star Wars,* Anakin Skywalker abandons the creed of the Jedi by adopting the ways of the dark side of the Force. He becomes a Sith Lord, Darth Vader, by discarding his insights into the good power of the Force and adopting the values of its evil counterpart, the Dark side. This can be considered a loss of Wisdom in the moralistic sense.

When Anakin first crosses over to the dark side, he arrives at a place of higher Power than the Underdogs but relatively lower Power than his new master, the Evil Emperor. Darth Vader becomes an Underling at this juncture.

As the dynamics of the conflicts in the *Star Wars* universe increase in further episodes, Darth Vader's character arc progresses again. He transitions into the primary antagonist, an Overlord—yet again another transformation of his role but this time happening from one story to another.

Of course, it's possible to make that jump to Overlord from Underling within the same novel. We'll discuss that character arc next.

The Underdog to Underling to Overlord transformation can certainly be executing within the same novel. Just make sure there's still a primary protagonist Underdog to take on the Overlord and complete the Hero's Journey.

Underling to Overlord

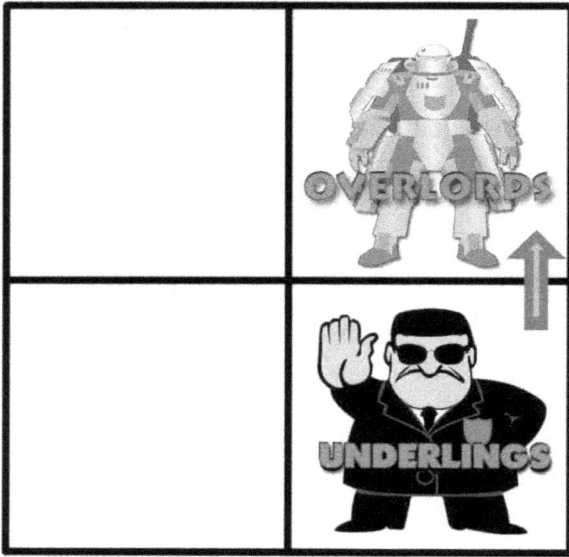

This character arc is very common. By the end of the story, one of the Underlings has assumed the mantle of the previous Overlord who may have fallen in battle or been usurped in a coup. The Underling replaces the dead king or queen or the deposed dictator or godfather by right of succession or from an act of conquest.

In *Star Wars*, Darth Vader transforms from Underling to Overlord. This can happen within a novel or by the end of a novel, setting up the sequel. In all cases, it is the acquisition of higher *relative* Power over the other characters that does the trick.

Character drives the plot, and the plot moulds the character's arc. — KM Weiland.

The literary elements of plot and character work interdependently. I encourage you to use The Character Quad as a tool to explore ways of planning and executing your character arcs both within a story and from one story to the next.

CHAPTER THIRTEEN

Conflicts and The Quad

Have you ever watched a TV series where even the best of friends or a tight circle of work colleagues get into the most incredible arguments?

Ugly debates and nasty disagreements. Interpersonal friction. Slanderous dialogue. People are chastised, bullied, stereotyped, looked down upon, harangued, and harassed. And this occurs between people who are supposed to like each other or work closely together!

Well, all of that verbal combat is the result of a screenwriter injecting conflict into what may be a rather dull scene without any.

I find most police and crime dramas on TV are like this. The detective's office or the forensics lab is never a sanctuary of peace and quiet. Someone is always disagreeing with someone else. The investigators' boss is always putting their foot down to get their way on how the investigation should proceed. The troops then push back and go against the boss's orders, setting up—yes, that's right—more conflict.

Soap operas depend almost entirely on conflict. Their popularity wouldn't exist without it. Even a comedy uses conflict to generate laughs.

Once you know why conflict is used so much on TV, you can never watch programs again without thinking... oh, no, not again... more conflict! Why? Because conflict is one of the best ways to hook an audience and drag them into the story.

K.M. Weiland in Creating Character Arcs:
'Characters... resist change just as staunchly as any of us—which is a good thing. Out of resistance comes conflict; out of conflict comes plot. This is just the first of many ways in which plot and character arcs are inextricable from one another.'

Conflict is an essential element in any story. Without conflict, stories lack drama.

We can very simply define conflict as 'something that's in opposition to something else'.

Authors and screenwriters use conflicts as 'hooks' to lure readers or the audience into their story. Once hooked, conflict keeps their readers or viewers connected to their characters by virtue of the emotional response created.

When readers experience conflict they become invested in your character's transformation (their arc) from the beginning of your story to the end, to see if your hero will prevail over adversity.

The more the story grabs your reader's attention, the better. The more emotional response you can generate in your readers, the better. This means, in general, the more conflict, the better.

The resolution of any or all of a story's conflicts becomes a big part of any character's Hero's Journey.

When I'm revising my own work, if a scene seems a little dull or slow-paced, it's often because there's a lack of conflict. By reflecting on which characters are in that scene, I look for opportunities to create conflict between them to resolve this problem and make the scene more dramatic.

It's surprising what else can come out of a simple injection of conflict. New ways of advancing the plot emerge or new ways to move someone along their character arc can occur.

Conflict is a great way to break through writer's block. Not sure where to go next? Create some conflict in the scene where you're stuck and see where that new conflict leads you!

So, let's look at how The Character Quad can help you generate opportunities to write conflict into your story.

Types of Conflict:

Characters in a fictional story can suffer from a variety of conflicts. The two overall categories are Internal Conflict and External Conflict.

Internal conflict, as it suggests, occurs from 'within'. This kind of conflict relates to a character's desires and motivations. In essence, this conflict is about the character battling his/her demons—the things in their personal nature that hold them back—their flaws, weaknesses, bad habits, and foibles. Internal conflicts act as psychological barriers that hinder the character's progress towards their goals.

When faced with adversity, or in critical moments of decision, these internal conflicts can push the character off track. They act in opposition to the character's journey and therefore limit success. The character must face these negative internal forces alone in order to overcome them.

External events have influence on internal conflicts but in the end, resolution of an internal conflict must come from within, usually by enacting a change that overcomes a weakness. Fearful characters must become brave. Flawed characters must not let their emotions, disabilities, or bad habits get in the way of their goals.

External conflict occurs between the character and some form of external force that is acting in opposition to their goals.

External conflicts can be further divided into:

(1) conflicts between one character and another

(2) conflicts that occur between the character and some external force or entity.

Examples of external forces that create conflict are technology (robots, AI, surveillance tech, etc), society (its norms and expectations), Nature (the environment, disasters, etc), or conflicts with some supernatural entity (ghosts, goblins, vampires, etc).

The Character Quad is a tool to help identify external conflicts that occur between characters.

Note: if you're writing about something that's not human like an android or a vampire, and you've assigned a character name to that entity, then of course, the Character Quad can be used to understand those kinds of conflicts as well. Your otherworldly entities should be treated as characters in the 'character to character' sense of conflict.

In an epic fantasy for example, none of the characters may be human at all—gollums, orcs, elves, etc.

In a science fiction novel, you may describe an extra-terrestrial as 'the Alien'; or create a name for a species of aliens like 'the Klingons', collective enemies in conflict with your protagonists.

As long as the external conflict is with 'something' that can be visualised as a character, you can place the name of that 'something' in one of the quadrants to identify the possible conflicts between that 'something' and your characters.

Conflicts Between Quadrants

When it comes to *character-to-character conflicts* there are Ten Conflict Interfaces in the Character Quad. Each represents a potential opportunity for conflict between types of characters in your story.

There are four interfaces between adjacent quadrants:

    Underdogs << >> Underlings

    Mentors << >> Overlords

    Underdogs << >> Mentors

    Overlords << >> Underlings

There are two through the center of the diagram:

Underdogs << >> Overlords

Mentors << >> Underlings

And there are four within each of the quadrants:

Underdogs << >> Underdogs

Overlords << >> Overlords

Mentors << >> Mentors

Underlings << >> Underlings

That's a lot from such a simple diagram!

As soon as you create your own Character Quads, you'll intuitively recognise these interfaces. Any boundary between one character's quadrant and another character's quadrant represents a potential opportunity to create conflict.

Underdogs << >> Overlords

The most important conflict interface by far is the conflict between the primary protagonist and the primary antagonist—represented by the conflict between an Underdog and an Overlord.

In *The Wizard of Oz* example, the conflict between Dorothy and the Wicked Witch is the primary conflict in the story.

Why? It's pretty obvious. Dorothy's journey is the primary Hero's Journey, the essence of the story. The Wicked Witch is her primary antagonist. Their conflict drives events to a resolution.

But let's not forget that other characters accompany Dorothy on her journey—the Scarecrow, the Tin Man, and the Cowardly Lion. As secondary characters, each of them has their own Journey. They are also Underdogs. And they also have conflicts with the Wicked Witch.

So, there are four Underdog to Overlord conflicts in the story, *The Wizard of Oz*. Four opportunities to create drama. Four opportunities to generate an emotional response in your reader.

This example shows that just because there may be six possible *interfaces* between the quadrants, it doesn't mean there are only six conflicts in the story.

The actual number of conflicts will depend on how many characters you have and what conflicts you want to create at the various interfaces with other characters.

How conflicts arise, with who, how they change, and how they influence events throughout your protagonist's journey are important elements to consider if you want to generate an emotional response that will hook your readers.

How many conflicts you have is your choice. Just don't overlook the opportunity, even if the conflict is minor.

The Blank Quadrant

What happens if you don't populate one of the quads with any characters?

Let's consider this example—you've chosen not to have any Underlings in your story. That's a legitimate choice. No one will argue with your decision not to have an Underling if that's what you think is best for your story.

For argument's sake, let's say you've chosen at least one Mentor in your story. Your Character Quad looks like this:

The Underling quadrant is blank. Is that a problem?
You are missing two important opportunities:

(1) a character that can influence your plot by interfering with the Hero's Journey.

(2) an opportunity to create drama through conflict with other characters.

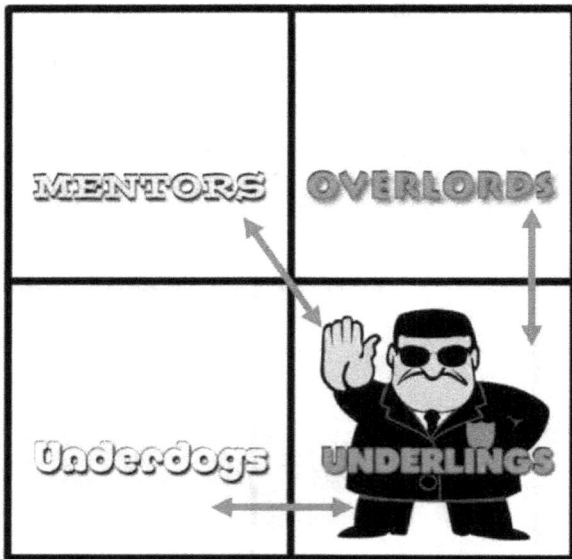

Your choice has resulted in three lost opportunities for conflict because these conflict interfaces don't exist:

Underlings << >> Underdogs

Underlings << >> Overlords

Underlings << >> Mentors

A single Underling can create at least three possible conflict interfaces, including arguably the most important two—with your primary Underdog hero and your primary Overlord.

If you have multiple characters in each of the other three quadrants, those lost opportunities multiply like rabbits.

Let's say you have two characters in each of the other three quadrants (Underdog, Overlord, Mentor)—representing a major and a minor character of each type— then you've missed *six* opportunities created by *six* possible conflict interfaces with just this *one* missing Underling character.

Increase your Underling count from one to two and potential conflict interfaces rise dramatically. If you have two Underlings and two characters in each of the other quadrants, you've now missed *twelve* opportunities for conflict represented by *twelve* possible character interfaces.

Another thing happens when you have two Underlings—they can have a conflict between themselves. This is the Underlings-to-Underlings interface.

Adding that interface increases the potential for new conflicts to a total of *thirteen*—and that's with only eight total characters in the entire story! Can you imagine if you had more? And how about new characters introduced in further novels in the series?

Carrying a single Underling over from one novel to the next would present new opportunities for conflict with new characters in later stories. That's a lot of missed opportunities!

Since each quadrant in The Character Quad represents a different combination of *relative* Power and *relative* Wisdom, the lack of any characters in the quadrants of Mentors and Underlings represents not just many lost opportunities for conflict but also many lost opportunities for different *types* of conflict.

This occurs because there are *relative* differences in Power and Wisdom between the two characters in question and these differences will influence the nature of the conflict.

There are so many ideas for conflict that spring from just one of these lost interfaces, it's hard to list all the examples resulting from the combinations created by these missed opportunities.

Certainly, a Mentor has a different profile of Power and Wisdom than an Underling. They are diametrically opposed. One has more Wisdom; the other more Power. What kind of conflict can your imagination create in that situation? The conflict between a Mentor and an Underling will have an entirely different nature than the conflict between a Mentor and your Underdog hero. But without an Underling in your story, you will never find out.

No one says you must have conflicts between each character. Many characters roles are minor. Some function as bit characters, part of the scenery.

We've discussed the impact conflict brings to your story—conflict hooks your readers. Interpersonal relationships generate a myriad of possibilities for writers, from love and friendship, to hate and nemesis. Granted, not all of these relationships will result in conflict. But then again, don't most lovers have quarrels?

In the end, the Character Quad can only offer suggested points of conflict. It's up to you to decide if you want them in your story.

We started this guide with the idea that a story needs to have at least two characters, a protagonist and an antagonist.

We discussed how a story with only these two roles would be very limited. One reason for that would be the single conflict interface between the two roles.

We discussed why other characters are needed to support the primary Underdog on their Hero's Journey and what roles they play, using the concepts of *relative* Power and *relative* Wisdom. More characters and the conflicts between them inevitably elicit more emotional response from your readers.

No one says you *must* have these extra characters in your story. However, I hope I've been able to demonstrate how the Character Quad helps you understand *why* they can have a profound effect on your story.

Each character creates a point of conflict with another.

Each character quadrant creates different types of conflict interfaces based on the *relative* Power and *relative* Wisdom between quadrants.

I've made the point that the more conflict, the better. If you ask...how can I do that?...then the Character Quad can help you find the answer.

The Character Quad provides you with a very simple visual reference to the interfaces between your characters and in turn, allows you to identify possible points of conflict. Since finding as many possible sources of conflict is useful, these examples show you how adding even one character to a quadrant can significantly multiply the opportunities you have to add conflict to your story.

CHAPTER FOURTEEN

Parachuting an Archetype into The Quad

By now you should be well equipped to create your own Character Quad. You know how simple it is to construct, what the axes mean, what the four quadrant roles are, and how to identify conflict interfaces.

So, you're ready to put pen to paper (oops, did it again) but you hesitate. You're still not sure if you'll be defying The Ancient Greek Laws of Archetypes. You're afraid that hellfire and brimstone will rain down from the literary gods if you dare ignore the Sacred Codex of Character Creation, the archetype.

What if an archetype you want to choose isn't a suitable candidate for use in the Character Quad?

Can I prove to you The Character Quad will not restrict your choice of archetype for any of your characters, regardless of which role you have chosen for them— Underdog, Mentor, Overlord, or Underling?

It's a legitimate question. If you still have lingering doubts about how The Character Quad can supplement the idea of archetypes, you want me to give you concrete proof. I don't blame you.

Let's climb Mount Olympus together and see what they've got. Bring it on, Zeus!

Oh, geez—don't we need a flying horse or a golden fleece or something? After all we'll be facing gods!

Okay, fear not.

We'll demonstrate the mortal powers of The Character Quad to the Gods of Archetype using a carefully designed experiment that hopefully won't piss them off.

Gulp. Do I have to come with you?

Yes, you do.

First step—let's open the aforementioned hallowed textbooks about archetypes and look through them again. Yes, the ones we dusted off at the beginning of this guide, quickly referenced, and just as quickly put back on the shelf. We will enlist these textbooks in our experiment.

Let's select two random examples of character archetypes from the textbooks—one female, one male—and parachute each one into our Character Quad like this:

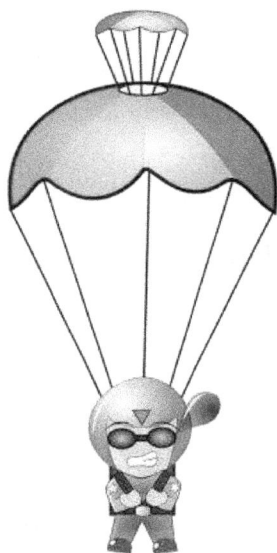

The aim of our experiment will be to use the same classical archetype to create a character to fit in *each* of the Quad's four quadrants.

To make it even more difficult, each of the four possible characters we will create from this single archetype must feature in the same general plot, to demonstrate to the Gods of Literature how *any* archetype can be used in a Character Quad for *any* role in *any* given novel we want to write.

All right then. Flying horse, it is! Count me in.

Good.

Ready? Let's get started...

Archetype Choice #1 — Hestia
The Mystic or The Betrayer (Female)

Our first experiment involves an archetype chosen from *45 Master Characters (Mythic Models for Creating Original Characters)* by Victoria Lynn Schmidt.

Each of this text's 45 master archetypes has a good and a bad side—in this case, Hestia is *The Mystic* when a heroine and *The Betrayer* when a villain.

Here's how the Hestia archetype is characterised by the author of *45 Master Characters*:

As *The Mystic*, she is a woman of peace and mysticism who has a calm quiet disposition and is sensitive and gentle-mannered. She likes to be alone with her thoughts and is at one with herself. She desires simplicity, values her home life and solitude. She's happiest in a studio or garden and is afraid of losing her private place. She's eccentric, not easily manipulated, and is motivated by a sense of order.

Her personality plays into the realm of the mystic and she may engage in meditation, divination, and the occult. She is an empath; is compassionate but wary of public places and crowds; and hates the spotlight and competition.

Her character arc is based on her need to be more assertive; to experience life; to be herself regardless of what others think; and to express her true spirit. Her flaws come from feeling alone in a crowd and from living inside her head. She is shy and timid, and a dreamer.

As her bad alter ego *The Betrayer*, Hestia's sunny disposition masks a monster. She is easily ignored by others at their peril. She can disguise her dark side and is possibly a sociopath.

She has no close relationships; is self-serving, an expert liar, and is socially inept. Rejection may make her lose control. One suggested story character might be 'the nice old lady who poisons her husband'.

Okay, we are suitably primed to parachute this Hestia archetype into our experiment. But I'm not keen on the name Hestia. Let's call her Sophia.

The doors open on our jump plane, we're over the drop zone, and we push her out. Here she goes—have a nice trip Sophia, don't forget to roll when you hit the ground.

The Underdog is Sophia

Sophia leads a quiet life painting landscapes. She lives in a beachfront mobile home situated on a small cove on the coast of California and values her privacy. She sells her paintings in an art and curio shop she owns in the nearby tourist town of Santa Fiesta and makes extra money performing tarot card readings.

A stranger comes to town. Sophia reads her tarot and it reveals a dark past and an even darker future. Sophia discovers the stranger is a property developer who has a nefarious record of acquiring prime land after the owners have mysteriously disappeared. Is Sophia this stranger's next victim?

The Overlord is Sophia

Sophia is a property developer who doesn't take no for an answer. Her last partner-husband once tried and he died mysteriously in a boating accident. His body was never found. That was husband number four. She's decided her love-life is forever over and she can now focus her intense internal energies on business. Her competitors have always underestimated her. She keeps a low profile while on the hunt for the next deal.

Santa Fiesta is a town stuck in a 1950's time-warp and Sophia targets it for her next flip. She arrives with a promise to donate funds to makeover the school's playground and build a medical clinic, a ploy she's used in the past to win over locals but she's never spent a cent before and doesn't plan to start now.

The problem she soon discovers is that no one in Santa Fiesta wants to sell. That's not a big problem for Sophia. After she's done with them, they'll be crawling on their hands and knees to offer her their properties—if they have hands and knees, that is. She spies her first victim, a local painter who lives on prime beachfront.

The Mentor is Sophia

Sophia is the town librarian in Santa Fiesta. She knows everyone who lives there and everything about the town from the time it was a mail stop on the Pony Express.

The town was founded by an eccentric millionaire who made his fortune in the California Gold Rush. Ownership of the land and the rights of property owners are mired in a labyrinth of special covenants enshrined in county bylaws that were created by his descendants to preserve it from over-development. As town librarian, she's studied those records and is the go-to adviser to a local lawyer whenever property is sold.

Sophia is a spinster who loves reading novels about the supernatural and lives alone in an old house next to the library. When a property developer disturbs the peaceful life of Santa Fiesta and threatens her friend, a local painter, Sophia rises to the occasion to help her friend fight back.

Little do they realise this is more than just a legal fight as one by one property owners die accidentally. Is her friend next? Sophia has a plan to help her.

The Underling is Sophia

Sophia, Santa Fiesta's appointed town clerk, keeps herself to herself in her eclectic old house filled with a collection of mystic objects and voodoo dolls. Her garden of roses is her pride and joy. She's nurtured them from seedlings as if they were her children. She was never married. Most of the townsfolk won't have anything to do with her socially and the feeling is mutual.

She lives in a tense but peaceful co-existence with her neighbours until a property developer comes to town that upsets her quiet little world. A war is breaking out and people are choosing sides.

The developer needs someone to help her navigate the local county bylaws and 'encourage' people to sell their properties. When a move to replace Sophia as town clerk is made by a clique who bear her a grudge, Sophia decides her best option is to dig into the covenants and find ways to screw them over. And it pays well. She's cut a sweetheart deal with the developer for every property she delivers up, using obscure legalities no one even knows exist.

How did Sophia do?

In all four of these roles, we can use the qualities, virtues, and flaws of the *Mystic/Betrayer* archetype to build our Sophia character regardless of her role.

Dialogue can exemplify her *Mystic* shyness, eccentricity, sensitivity, and gentle manners, while as *The Betrayer*, she can be shown to lie and lose control when rejected.

Sophia's occupation as either painter or librarian uses her *Mystic* empathy and compassion to further the plot but as *The Betrayer*, her property developer Overlord or town clerk Underling are sociopathic monsters hiding behind empathetic facades.

In any of the four roles, we can put Sophia in situations that show her wariness of public places and crowds. We can show how she would react when put in the spotlight or when faced with competition.

The traits of her archetype and her responses to her environment are independent of Sophia's role in this novel's Character Quad.

Archetype Choice #2
The Professor (Male)

Our second experiment involves an archetype chosen from *The Complete Writer's Guide to Heroes and Heroines* by Cowden, LaFever, and Viders—*The Professor.*

In this instance, no guidance is offered that indicates any good/bad duality with this archetype. We therefore must assume the qualities, virtues, and flaws of *The Professor* apply equally in both cases of hero or villain.

We need to give *The Professor* a name. Let's call him Pavel.

According to *The Complete Writer's Guide to Heroes and Heroines,* Pavel's archetype is logical, introverted, and faithful. His strength is his intellect, special skills, and expertise. He has all the answers; he's analytical and objective. He could be characterised as suffering from obsessive-compulsive disorder and is a slave to logic. He is inflexible, set in his ways, and not very enthusiastic about change.

Pavel thinks his way is always best. Because of this, Pavel finds it hard to communicate on other peoples' levels which frustrates him. But Pavel is also genuine, vulnerable, and neither a hypocrite or a liar. He is insular, unwilling to make room for others, and not knowledgeable outside his expertise. He's a poor socialiser and uncomfortable in the presence of the opposite sex. Needless to say, all of this means he's not the life of any party.

According to *The Professor* archetype, Pavel can appear in our novel in two very contrasting styles. He can either be an absent-minded lovable klutz with messy hair and dress; or conversely, seen as super-organised and immaculately turned out. At first glance, these visual opposites present us with a perplexing dilemma—what to choose? But on the other hand, it gives us several degrees of freedom as we parachute Pavel *the Professor* into our Character Quad.

Let's find out how he does. Pavel exits the plane. Here he goes:

The Underdog is Pavel

Pavel toils in the coding department of a high-tech startup whose newest product has captured the interest of the Pentagon. It's a facial recognition system called CyberTruth that acts like a visual lie-detector, a highly powerful tool that can root out spies and traitors within the military and diplomatic world.

But Pavel has discovered CyberTruth's algorithm has other potentially devious uses. The program can characterise a person's political leanings and sexual preferences with uncanny accuracy with a simple facial scan. A surveillance program like this would leave everyone it targets open to political oppression, blackmail, and intimidation. In the wrong hands, CyberTruth can tear society apart and help a dictator come to power, even in one of the world's largest democracies.

Pavel, a scruffy OCD nerd, has few friends and is a slave to his work. He's not political but understands that CyberTruth's algorithm as an artificial intelligence is apolitical and in the wrong hands could be dangerous. This inconvenient truth needs to come out before the small company is sold to a big social media corporation.

Pavel turns whistle-blower and enlists the aid of an investigative journalist. Soon the pair find they are the targets of powerful forces that will stop at nothing to keep CyberTruth's dark side from being exposed.

The Overlord is Pavel

Pavel is the CEO of tech startup CyberTruth, a company he founded in his basement. He's devoted his whole career obsessing over code to the detriment of any social life.

It's been a long, lonely struggle to get his brainchild recognised by venture capitalists who are now falling over themselves to bankroll his completed project, a uniquely powerful facial recognition system. His newfound wealth is daunting and he's uncomfortable with the party lifestyle that comes with it.

At one of these parties, Pavel learns a member of his coding team is about to expose a dark secret about CyberTruth—if a module Pavel once developed is inserted in the code, CyberTruth's capabilities can be exploited for evil.

Pavel must identify who knows this secret and stop him or her—in any way he can—from destroying his dream.

The Mentor is Pavel

Pavel is an investigative journalist who earns a meagre income freelancing from his cramped office in a small rented basement apartment. Life is hard; his clothes are threadbare and his shoes have holes in them.

He has no social life but when he gets interested in a corporate cover-up or a juicy political scandal, he throws his body and soul into the investigation and that really turns him on. He has his own way of doing things which aggravates the news editors he works with, but they like his results. One of them refers a whistle-blower to Pavel— a computer programmer at tech startup CyberTruth that is about to unveil a new facial recognition software program.

Pavel meets with the coder and discovers the truth behind CyberTruth. The coder receives threatening messages and soon the pair realise no one in the coder's world can be trusted. Pavel has lived in the shadows long enough to know how to hide from scrutiny and helps his new charge go off-grid until they can gather the proof they need to go public.

The Underling is Pavel

Pavel's OCD has destroyed every relationship he's ever had. His neatness obsession—never wearing the same tie twice, dry-cleaning unworn suits if they show even a tiny speck of lint, cataloguing every object in his apartment—has eventually driven away every one of his girlfriends.

But he's finally found a well-paid job that uses this disorder to his advantage. Pavel is a personal assistant to a high-flying but disorganised serial entrepreneur who's just bought startup CyberTruth. His boss leans on Pavel to sweat the details of his complicated fast-paced lifestyle, a skill Pavel is exceedingly good at. As long as the money keeps rolling in, Pavel's life is good.

But something is about to upset the applecart—a whistle-blower that threatens to ignite a stack of dynamite under CyberTruth's future. Pavel is tasked by his ruthless boss to root out this saboteur—if Pavel can find out who it is. Pavel uses all his skills as an ex-CIA analyst to lay the groundwork for some devious traps. Whatever his boss wants, Pavel is determined to deliver.

How did Pavel do?

In all four of these examples, we have used the qualities, virtues, and flaws of *The Professor* archetype to build our Pavel character regardless of which role we've chosen to put him in the Character Quad.

Dialogue can exemplify Pavel's introverted OCD; his insular nature and inflexibility; his overbearing manner of thinking his way is always best; and his frustration at not being able to communicate on other people's level. These traits are independent of his role in the Character Quad.

The occupation chosen for each of his roles can demonstrate his analytical skills, intellect, and expertise and help move the plot forward. His character arc can show his vulnerability and his slavishly-flawed devotion to logic.

It doesn't matter if Pavel is the Underdog whistle-blower, the scruffy journalist Mentor, the dispassionate Overlord entrepreneur, or the devious OCD Underling assistant. We can weave *The Professor's* character traits into any role we choose as we parachute *The Professor* into this novel's Character Quad.

Will the Gods of Archetype be suitably impressed with our demonstration of Character Quad power?

It's not the Gods you need to impress—it's your reader.

When it comes to character building and development, you need to use all of the available tools. The Character Quad isn't magic and it's not a false king. It works in concert with archetypes, character arc, and conflict to help you build the best characters for your story, regardless of their role.

CHAPTER FIFTEEN

Summary - Final Words

Lets' summarise what we've learned about The Character Quad:

(1) The Character Quad is a tool that helps you answer two questions other tools don't:

What kinds of characters does my story need?
How many characters does my story need?

(2) We can choose any archetype we want and position them in the Quad by virtue of their *relative* Power and *relative* Wisdom. The Character Quad is not a replacement for archetypes. It can work with any archetype you choose from any text. By leveraging the concepts of *relative* Power and *relative* Wisdom with any archetype's personality traits, qualities, and flaws the only limit is your imagination.

(3) The Character Quad supplements the concept of the Hero's Journey by helping you identify and manage roles for the main and secondary characters along the way.

(4) The Character Quad doesn't replace the character arc—it supplements it by showing you how to change your characters' *relative* Power and *relative* Wisdom as they grow in the story. Character arcs are a dynamic interaction of character and plot. Characters will change throughout your story both in terms of where they started their Hero's Journey; how they change in relation to other characters; and how everyone ends up. As characters grow, it ultimately leads to a resolution of their inner and external journeys. The Character Quad helps you visualise your character arcs by providing possibilities and choices for character growth through changes in *relative* Power and *relative* Wisdom.

(5) The Character Quad helps you identify conflict interfaces which are opportunities to add drama in order to hook your readers. The Character Quad's construction using the ideas of *relative* Wisdom and *relative* Power allows you to manage the interpersonal dynamics between pairs of characters. The Character Quad shows you potential opportunities for conflict as characters

interact and offers routes to write conflict into your story while allowing many degrees of freedom and choice to add conflict or to leave it out.

(6) By populating The Character Quad with major, minor, and bit characters, we can visually see if there is a good balance of character roles and quickly identify if any quadrant is either under- or over-populated.

(7) The Character Quad provides a handy reference to your initial and subsequent character lists as you grow your character universe into a series of novels. You can elect to turn minor characters into major ones, transition characters from one Quad role to another, and elevate bit characters into higher roles.

I hope you've seen how beneficial The Character Quad can be as a valuable tool in your writer's repertoire!

CHAPTER SIXTEEN

The Character Quad Template

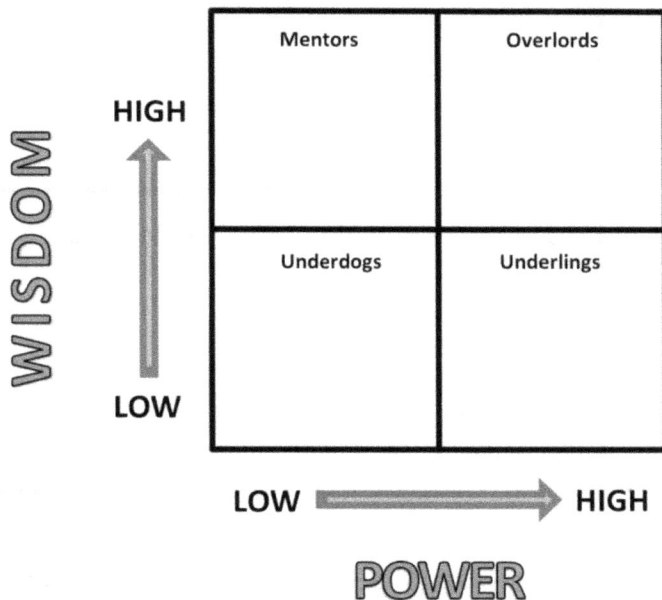

	Mentors	Overlords
HIGH ↑ WISDOM ↓ **LOW**		
	Underdogs	Underlings

LOW ⟹ HIGH

POWER

But this is all you really need—
a simple Two X Two Table like this:

Mentors	Overlords
Underdogs	Underlings

I promised The Character Quad would be simple to construct and simple to use—if you think I delivered, please share your thoughts and write a review! It would be very much appreciated.

Thank you! — *Charles A Cornell*

Book Two: Exploring the Quad

Well, that's it—you're now completely ready to use The Character Quad as a tool to develop characters for your stories. It's a simple concept to learn and should be simple to use.

The best way to get proficient is to put it into action. As you do, you'll no doubt discover a whole host of valuable applications to enhance your stories and that means you may have further questions.

I've developed a second guide for advanced users of The Character Quad called *Exploring The Quad.*

After using The Character Quad for the first time, you will want to come back to learn even more about how The Character Quad applies in different situations and with different genres.

In Book Two—*Exploring The Quad*—we will put The Character Quad through its paces again and examine the results in a variety of character-building situations.

In Part I of *Exploring The Quad*—we will discuss how to build your character universe. We'll review additional examples from popular culture as well as take a real-life look at a specific novel series with hundreds of characters, as it evolved, book by book. What choices did the author make and why?

We will see how to use The Character Quad to refresh an existing character list. We will refine our definitions of major and minor characters. *Exploring The Quad* will demonstrate the value of resurrecting forgotten characters and discuss the 'how and when' of killing characters off.

We'll examine how The Character Quad can help you write stories told from multiple perspectives with multiple protagonists, and how it is used to write an Anti-Hero or an Anti-Villain.

We'll examine the role of characters that your other characters never meet—intrigued? And conversely, how to assign roles to characters that feature in live-action situations but are never given formal names—*say what*? Don't fear, answers await.

In Part II of *Exploring The Quad*—we will explore conflict in greater depth, showing not only how to use the conflict interfaces identified by The Character Quad in one novel but over a series of novels as you build your character universe.

In Part III of *Exploring The Quad*—we will delve further into the relationship between character and plot and examine additional ways the Character Quad can help develop character arcs as your stories progress from one novel to the next.

Recommended Reference Texts

45 Master Characters (Mythic Models for Creating Original Characters) — Victoria Lynn Schmidt

The Complete Writer's Guide to Heroes and Heroines — Cowden, LaFever, and Viders

Dynamic Characters: How To Create Personalities That Keep Readers Captivated — Nancy Kress

Characters and Viewpoint — Orson Scott Card, part of the Writer's Digest series on Elements of Fiction Writing

The Hero with a Thousand Faces — Joseph Campbell

Creating Character Arcs: The Masterful Author's Guide to Uniting Story Structure, Plot, and Character Development — KM Weiland

Snakes in Suits: Understanding and Surviving the Psychopaths in Your Office — Dr. Paul Babiak and Dr. Robert D. Hare

About the Author – Charles A Cornell

When Charles isn't trying to survive the chaos of everyday life, he's dreaming up speculative fiction ranging from the mysterious to the macabre, often blending science fiction with fantasy and alternative history. His goal is to thrill and amaze his readers with dynamic plots, unusual twists, interesting characters, and worlds of wonder. He's a regular contributor to podcasts, seminars and conferences, and conducts webinars and workshops on his specialty, retro-punk fiction (Steampunk, Dieselpunk).

His novels and short fiction have won numerous Gold Medals from the Royal Palm Literary Awards of the Florida Writers Association. His short stories feature in seven anthologies.

Charles lives in a rural English village in Lincolnshire, England with his wife and a ginger tabby who claims to be from another dimension and will push his master through a wormhole if he's not fed on demand.

Websites:

Cornell-SciFi.com

CharlesACornell.com

SteampunkNovels.com

DragonFly-Novels.com

Fiction by Charles A. Cornell

Novels

    Tiger Paw (Mystery Thriller)

    DragonFly (Science Fantasy / Dieselpunk)

Coming Soon: Astragenesis (SciFi Novel Series)

    Reborn / Resist / Reclaim

Speculative Fiction Short Stories

    The Most Peculiar Tales (Steampunk Anthology)

    Crystal Night (The Prometheus Saga Vol 1)

    The Orchid Man (The Prometheus Saga Vol 2)

    Children Of The Stars (Return To Earth)

    The Scream (The Masters Reimagined Vol 2)

    The Factory (In Shadows Written)

    Andromeda Calling (The Light Fantastic)

    SOD's Law (The Light Fantastic)

Non-Fiction

    A Survivor's Guide To Working At A Big Corporation

Satire

    Harvey Drinkwater and The Cult Of Savings